NEW VANGUARD 322

US NAVY GUN DESTROYERS 1945–88

Fletcher class to Forrest Sherman class

MARK STILLE   ILLUSTRATED BY ADAM TOOBY

OSPREY PUBLISHING

Bloomsbury Publishing Plc

Kemp House, Chawley Park, Cumnor Hill, Oxford OX2 9PH, UK

29 Earlsfort Terrace, Dublin 2, Ireland

1385 Broadway, 5th Floor, New York, NY 10018, USA

E-mail: info@ospreypublishing.com

www.ospreypublishing.com

OSPREY is a trademark of Osprey Publishing Ltd

First published in Great Britain in 2023

A catalog record for this book is available from the British Library.

ISBN: PB 9781472855121; eBook 9781472855145; ePDF 9781472855152; XML 9781472855138

23 24 25 26 27 10 9 8 7 6 5 4 3 2 1

Index by Fionbar Lyons
Typeset by PDQ Digital Media Solutions, Bungay, UK
Printed and bound in India by Replika Press Private Ltd.

Osprey Publishing supports the Woodland Trust, the UK's leading woodland conservation charity.

To find out more about our authors and books visit www.ospreypublishing.com. Here you will find extracts, author interviews, details of forthcoming events and the option to sign up for our newsletter.

Author's note

Abbreviations used in this book:

AAW – Antiair warfare

ASROC – Antisubmarine rocket

ASW – Antisubmarine warfare

BS – Battle star

CG – Guided-missile cruiser

CLK – Sub-killer cruiser

CR – Campaign ribbon

DD – Destroyer

DDK – Destroyer submarine killer

DDR – Radar picket destroyer

DDG – Guided-missile destroyer

DL – Destroyer leader (later reclassified as frigate)

DMS – Minelayer

DASH – Drone antisubmarine helicopter

ECM – Electronic countermeasures

FRAM – Fleet Rehabilitation and Modernization

FY – Fiscal year

HF/DF – High frequency direction finding

Mk – Mark

SAM – Surface-to-air missile

SCB – Ship Construction Board

USN – US Navy

VDS – Variable depth sonar

All photos courtesy of the Naval History and Heritage Center.

CONTENTS

US NAVY GUN DESTROYERS 1945–88

Fletcher class to Forrest Sherman class

INTRODUCTION

Many of the Fletchers that returned to service during the Korean War received almost no modernization. This is *Bradford* at sea around 1961. The ship retains its full battery of five 5in/38 guns and a bank of torpedo tubes. Its ASW battery has been slightly upgraded with the fitting of Mk 10 or 11 Hedgehog launchers abreast the bridge. All the depth charge projectors have been removed and only a single rack remains on the stern. A new tripod mast has been added with the SPS-6 and SPS-10 radars. *Bradford* received six battle stars for service off Korea.

The United States Navy (USN) of the early Cold War period was the most powerful naval force on the planet. The most numerous combatants in this global fleet were its force of destroyers. After a prodigious World War II construction program, the USN was left with a huge number of destroyers. Of these, only the Fletcher, Sumner, and Gearing classes were considered suitable for continued service. The most important destroyer class of World War II, the Fletcher class, was built in enormous numbers – a total of 175 units. Few of these were kept in service immediately after the war, but during the Korean War the USN had 100 Fletcher-class units in service. Eighteen of these received a modernization to increase their effectiveness as antisubmarine warfare (ASW) escorts and another 40 received a minor upgrade to their antiair warfare (AAW) and ASW capabilities. The last Fletcher-class unit did not leave service until 1972.

The follow-on to the Fletcher class was the Sumner class of 58 units. The Sumner class shared the same size hull as the Fletcher class but was more heavily armed. A total of 53 saw service in the Cold War. All but seven of these served into the 1970s after receiving ASW and habitability upgrades. The final Sumner-class destroyer left USN service in 1975.

The Gearing class was the ultimate development of the Fletcher class. A total of 93 Gearings were produced to the original destroyer design, and five more were completed after the war. Because they underwent extensive modernization and served as late as 1983, the Gearing class was the predominate type of destroyer in the USN's Cold War fleet.

Shortly after World War II a single class of large "destroyer

leaders" was built. This was the four-ship Mitscher class; however, they proved too expensive for mass production. Even larger was the unique but unsuccessful *Norfolk*, built as a sub-killing cruiser.

As the World War II destroyers aged, the USN began to design a new class of gun destroyers. The final gun destroyer design was the Forrest Sherman class. The first ship of the USN's ultimate expression of an all-gun destroyer was laid down in 1953; eventually 18 entered service. Of these, only six remained in an all-gun configuration with the others receiving major ASW and AAW modifications during their careers.

The gun destroyers of all classes were the forgotten ships of the USN's Cold War operations. As the most numerous combatants in the fleet, they served all over the world and saw action in two wars and many other hot spots. By the 1960s they were unable to handle modern submarine and airborne threats and were gradually replaced by more capable units designed with greater ASW and AAW capabilities. Even after leaving USN service, the Fletcher, Sumner, and Gearing classes continued to serve all over the world in many different foreign navies.

BELOW LEFT
This view of *Fred T. Berry* in 1947 shows a Gearing-class unit in its as-built configuration. The only difference between a Gearing and the preceding Sumners was a 14ft extension amidships. *Berry* received a late-war antiaircraft upgrade so carries three 5in twin mounts, one bank of torpedo tubes, 16 40mm guns in three quad and two twin mounts, and ten 20mm mounts.

BELOW RIGHT
This is *Mitscher* in 1953 as it was completed. The ship's main weapons are clearly seen – two 5in/54 single mounts, two 3in/50 mounts, and two Weapon Alphas. Note the large SPS-8 height-finding radar abaft the second funnel.

USN COLD WAR DESTROYER DESIGNS

The first USN destroyer designed without any reference to treaty limitations was the Fletcher class. This translated into ships with adequate room to retain a main battery of five 5in guns and ten torpedo tubes and accept an increase in 40mm and 20mm antiaircraft guns. The design was so successful that 175 were built – the most by far of any USN destroyer class. Only 21 were lost during the war, so there were still huge numbers available after the war. Since they were big enough to accept modernization, it was envisioned that all the Fletchers would be converted to ASW escorts to deal with the large submarine force the Soviet Navy was expected to build.

In 1946–47, almost all the surviving Fletchers were placed in reserve. By 1950, only five were active as training ships assigned to the Naval Reserve. Eighteen were being modernized to DDEs, with all others being maintained as mobilization reserves. The Korean War, which began in June 1950, brought a massive increase in naval funding and the need for additional ships in service. This prompted the eventual reactivation of 100 Fletchers into USN service. Of the ships not converted into DDEs, 40 received an upgrade of their armament that replaced the wartime 40mm guns with the

 EARLY COLD WAR FLETCHER AND SUMNER CONFIGURATIONS

1. Fletcher-class ship in 1959. The top view depicts *Cogswell*, one of the 40 Fletcher-class units that were rearmed in the early 1950s. This is the ship as it appeared in 1959. It retains its basic World War II appearance since it still has four single 5in/38 mounts and one quintuple bank of torpedoes. All of the wartime 40mm and 20mm guns have been removed. In their place are three 3in/50 mounts with the aft one replacing the Number 3 5in/38 mount. On the new tripod mast is a SPS-6C air search radar and a SPS-10 surface search radar – this was the standard destroyer radar suite in the 1950s. Note the Hedgehog launchers abreast the modified bridge. The ship is in Design Measure 27 – Haze Gray System which was the common USN Cold War paint scheme.

2. A Sumner-class unit in 1953. This is *Lyman K. Swenson* in 1953 during its service in the Korean War. The Sumner rearmament program kept the World War II configuration of the class with fairly minor modifications. The three 40mm quad mounts have been replaced by two twin 3in/50 mounts and two single 3in/50 guns placed abeam the forward stack. All the 20mm guns have also been removed; two Hedgehog launchers replaced those 20mm guns formerly located abreast the bridge. The new tripod mast carries the SPS-6 and SPS-10 radars. Other new electronics include a Mk 25 radar on the Mk 37 fire control director located abaft the bridge and a Mk 56 fire control director abaft the second stack. *Lyman K. Swenson* gained six Battle Stars for its operations off Korea and then went on to make seven wartime deployments off Vietnam.

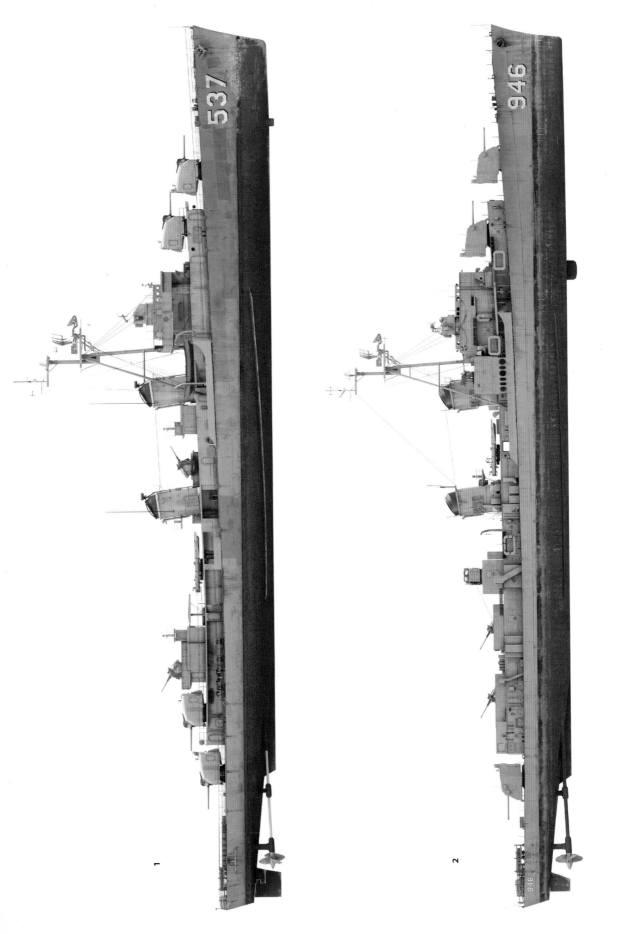

1

2

new 3in/50 twin mounts. This left 42 ships basically unmodified from their wartime configuration. These units received slight modifications before being retired in the 1950s and early 1960s. The rearmed ships and the DDEs served into the 1970s with the last ship being retired in 1972.

As successful as the Fletcher class was overall, it was deficient in certain areas. The ships were very wet forward, failed to meet their design speed as weight increased, and did not handle well. Successor to the Fletcher class was the Sumner–Gearing class. The Sumner class kept the same dimensions as the Fletcher class but possessed a slightly larger beam. This allowed the fitting of a heavier main battery arranged in three twin gun mounts. Two were placed forward of the bridge creating a much heavier weight of firepower forward. Eventually 58 were completed even though this was considered an interim design until an "ultimate" destroyer design could be completed. In addition to the heavier main battery of six 5in/38 guns, the Sumners' torpedo battery remained at ten tubes and their antiaircraft battery included more 40mm guns. The USN considered the Sumner class more effective than the Fletcher class but their extra weight resulted in a noticeable loss of speed.

The ultimate USN World War II destroyer design was the Gearing class. These were simply Sumner-class units with the addition of a 14ft section. The extra space was used primarily for fuel bunkerage which increased endurance from 3,300nm to 4,500nm. The same machinery and armament were retained from the Sumner class. The Gearing class was the ultimate development of the successful Fletcher-class design. The fact that eventually 98 Gearings were completed made them the most important USN Cold War destroyer and a stalwart in operations into the 1980s.

The USN flirted with large destroyer designs in the early Cold War period. Given the postwar supremacy of the USN and the low probability of fighting enemy surface forces, any new destroyer had to be designed to handle air and submarine attack. This supremacy also mitigated against large expenditures on destroyers when so many war-built units were available. To achieve the kind of capabilities desired, the new destroyer was going to be large. It turned out to be so large that it was clearly impossible to build them in large numbers. Four of these large destroyers were laid down beginning in 1949. They constituted the Mitscher class. The size of the new ships led to the designation as destroyer leaders and then as frigates (DL). They displaced almost 5,000 tons full load and were fitted with the new 5in/54 guns. They were the first ships fitted with the new 1,200lb 950-degree boilers which proved troublesome during their careers.

Forrest Sherman, lead ship of the USN's last class of gun destroyers, was a beautiful ship with its hurricane bow, two uneven stacks, and three 5in/54 mounts.

In keeping with its duties as an ASW test ship, *Norfolk* had both aft Weapon Alphas removed and replaced by the first ASROC launcher. Ultimately the design for a large and expensive ASW hunter-killer was a failure and *Norfolk* was decommissioned after only 17 years in service.

The Fleet Rehabilitation and Modernization (FRAM) Program

The huge numbers of destroyers built during or right after World War II – the Fletcher, Sumner, and Gearing classes – were becoming worn out by the late 1950s. Many ships had been in constant and arduous service since 1945. Cost precluded replacements, so the USN decided to rebuild many of them to extend their service lives. This became the Fleet Rehabilitation and Modernization (FRAM) program. Many Fletcher-class ships were scheduled to receive FRAM work but funding was limited and the Navy decided to focus on extending the lives of the more valuable Sumner and Gearing classes. The work was very extensive, taking nine to ten months per ship. The ships were torn down to the main deck level and also received an extensive internal refurbishment and machinery overhaul.

The FRAM I program was focused on the Gearing class. It featured a "complete rehabilitation of all shipboard components (hull and machinery) which will extend the useful life by about 8 years." Warfare systems were also improved. The ineffective 3in/50 gun mounts were removed, as was one of the 5in/38 twin mounts. FRAM I work focused on improving the ships' ASW capabilities – two Mk 32 triple torpedo launchers were added along with an ASROC launcher between the stacks; drone antisubmarine helicopter (DASH) facilities were fitted abaft the second stack; and a new SQS-23 sonar was fitted. Electronic countermeasures (ECM) equipment was added on top of the DASH hangar. In the new superstructure, an enlarged Combat Information Center (CIC) was built. Additional air conditioning was added to spaces for improved habitability. New air search and surface search radars were added. Both stacks were extended and capped, which became a defining characteristic of ships that had received FRAM work. A total of 79 Gearing DDs and DDRs received FRAM I modernization.

Perry was the first Gearing to undergo FRAM I work. This is *Perry* in January 1964 after modernization. As one of the first FRAM I conversions, *Perry* was completed as a Group A unit. Both forward 5in/38 mounts were retained, and the aft 5in/38 mount was removed and a pair of Mk 32 torpedo tubes placed aft. Heavy seas made it difficult to operate the Mk 32, so later ships had them moved forward in place of the Number 2 5in/38 mount.

FRAM II work focused primarily on Sumner-class ships. It was intended to extend the life of these ships by five years. The three 5in/38 mounts were retained, but the 3in/50 mounts were removed. ASW capabilities were upgraded with the addition of DASH facilities, two Mk 10 or Mk 11 Hedgehog projectors, two fixed Mk 25 torpedo tubes, two Mk 32 torpedo launchers, the SQS-4 sonar, and a variable depth sonar (VDS). Internal machinery was reworked as on the FRAM I ships. The forward superstructure was not completely rebuilt as on FRAM I ships, but new radars were added on the new tripod mast. These ships did not receive ASROC launchers since they were 14ft shorter than the Gearings. Altogether, three Fletchers, 33 Sumners, and 16 Gearings received this work.

The FRAM program proved very successful, primarily because it was much cheaper than buying new ships. FRAM I work cost $11 million per ship and FRAM II $7 million. Ships receiving this work served well beyond the five or eight additional years planned for. It forestalled the USN's block obsolescence for its destroyer force until after the Vietnam War.

Richard B. Anderson and another destroyer undergoing FRAM I modernization at Puget Sound Naval Shipyard in about 1960. Both destroyers were FRAM I Group A ships as indicated by the presence of both forward 5in/38 mounts. This photo shows the extent of FRAM modernization.

The expensive failure of the Mitscher-class design led to the return to a more traditional destroyer suited for potential wartime production. The design that eventually became the Forrest Sherman class was smaller and emphasized firepower over ASW capability. On a fairly small displacement, the ships carried three of the new 5in/54 guns in single mounts and two twin 3in/50 mounts, and had a radius of 4,600nm. One of the points of design emphasis was high speed. The USN preferred a destroyer capable of speeds high enough to have the necessary speed to act as part of the screen for carrier task forces. This was calculated to be 38kt, speeds the Fletchers, Sumners, and Gearings were incapable of. Initially, it was calculated that this speed could be achieved on a ship with a 2,500-ton displacement. This proved to be overly optimistic and the final design of the USN's last class of gun destroyer only managed 33kt on a hull of 2,850 tons.

The last ship to be considered is the unique *Norfolk*. This large ship was an ASW ship and not really a traditional destroyer design. It was based on a wartime cruiser hull. The design maximized ASW to allow it to perform as a submarine killer of the most advanced submarines of the day. Not completed until 1953, it was far too expensive for serial production. As a one-of-a-kind design, it spent its career as an experimental ship.

USN COLD WAR DESTROYER WEAPONS

Guns

Cold War destroyers were equipped with a number of gun systems. All were dual-purpose, capable of engaging air and surface targets. The 5in/38 gun dated from the early 1930s. It was renowned for its reliability and high rate of fire if operated by a well-trained crew. Beginning with the Mitscher class, it was replaced by the automatic 5in/54 Mk 42 mount that was complex and subject to jamming. After a series of modifications and a reduction in the rate of fire, the gun earned a reputation for reliability. Most Cold War destroyers carried the 3in/50 Mk 33 mount which was not available until 1947. It was developed as a replacement for the 40mm Bofors gun to combat the kamikaze threat. The shell fired by this gun was large enough to carry a proximity fuze which made it much more effective. However, during development the new gun gained weight and could not replace the 40mm mounts on a one-for-one basis. It was also difficult to maintain and proved unable to handle high-speed targets. These factors led to the disappearance of the 3in/50 gun from USN destroyers. The 3in/70 Mk 37 mount was intended to replace the 3in/50, but it too was plagued by maintenance problems because of its complexity and the lack of trained personnel to operate and maintain it. The wartime 40mm and 20mm guns remained on destroyers during the early period of the Cold War.

Forrest Sherman-class destroyer *Turner Joy* firing one of its three 5in/54 Mk 42 gun mounts at enemy positions in Vietnam in June 1968. After initial problems, the Mk 42 mount became a reliable weapon. Shore bombardment was the main task of the USN's older destroyers during the Cold War.

USN destroyer guns			
System	Shell size	Rate of fire	Maximum range
5in/38	54lb	15–20rpm	18,200yds
5in/54 Mk 42	70lb	40rpm (changed to 28 in 1968)	25,909yds
3in/50	34lb	45–50rpm	14,600yds
3in/70	36lb	90rpm	19,500yds
40mm	2lb	160rpm	11,000yds
20mm	0.27lb	450rpm	4,800yds

Missiles

Missiles were only deployed on a few of the ships in this book, so their development will be traced briefly. One Gearing was used to prove the practicability of deploying the Terrier surface-to-air-missile (SAM) system on smaller ships. It was an austere conversion with the Terrier launcher replacing the aft 5in/38 twin mount. The Mk 25 radar used to control the 5in guns was used as a missile control radar. The conversion was not a success and *Gyatt* reverted to a regular destroyer within a few years.

Since Terrier was too large for small ships, a new requirement was issued for a smaller SAM. This became the Tartar SAM system and was deployed on the Mitscher- and Forrest Sherman-class DDG conversions. Though early versions were unreliable, the RIM-24C version could engage targets out to 17.5nm.

Torpedoes

The USN's standard World War II destroyer torpedo was the Mk 15; it was designed to attack surface targets. This 21in diameter weapon had three speed settings – 26.5kt out to 15,000yds; 33kt for 10,000yds; 45kt for 6,000yds. It carried a warhead of 800lb. During the Cold War, the USN saw little practical use for these weapons against enemy surface targets, but the torpedo tubes were reserved for a future heavyweight ASW torpedo that never came into service.

ASW weapons

Given their mission, every USN destroyer carried ASW weapons. The standard World War II ASW weapon was the depth charge deployed over the stern or on each beam by projectors. Depth charges were short-ranged and inaccurate, and possessed a small lethal radius. This led to their removal from USN destroyers during the Cold War. During World War II, the thrown-ahead Hedgehog system was deployed on ASW escorts but only had a range of about

Gyatt as seen in its guided missile destroyer configuration in 1956 with the Terrier SAM system aft. The following year it was reclassified DDG 1. The experiment to put the Terrier on a destroyer-sized ship was a failure, and the system was removed and *Gyatt* was reclassified as a destroyer in 1962. It was one of three Gearings not to receive FRAM work.

Mitscher-class frigate *Wilkinson* fires a Weapon Alpha in about 1956. This weapon was an ultimately unsuccessful attempt to provide early Cold War ASW ships with a stand-off weapon to counter modern submarines. Note the 5in/54 Mk 42 mount in the foreground.

200yds. The fixed Mk 10 or Mk 11 Hedgehog was the first Cold War upgrade for most USN destroyers. The Mk 11 deployed its charges in an elliptical pattern 280yds in advance of the ship. Postwar versions of the Hedgehog included the trainable Mk 14 and the Mk 15, which was also stabilized and trainable. The Hedgehog was judged to be inadequate against the new generation of submarines and was gradually removed during the Cold War. To replace it, the USN developed a weapon with a greater stand-off range – the Mk 108 Weapon Alpha. This was a depth charge projector that fired a 12.75in ASW rocket. It was installed in a stabilized and trainable mount with its own fire control system. Weapon Alpha had a range of about 800yds and could fire 12rpm, but only had 22 rounds in its ready magazine. Reliability and maintenance issues, combined with its short range, led to it also being removed from service.

ASW homing torpedoes promised more range and effectiveness. The first was the Mk 24 that proved effective during World War II. The Mk 24 became the Mk 32 lightweight torpedo which was launched from a set of rails, not from a tube. The last generation of lightweight active torpedoes, the Mk 44 and 46, was fired from the Mk 32 lightweight torpedo tube. The Mk 44 began production in 1963. It was replaced by the Mk 46, which was faster (45kt) and could dive deeper. The USN also attempted to deploy the full size (21in) Mk 35 active torpedo on surface ships, and Mk 25 tubes were fitted on several classes of destroyers in expectation of these weapons being deployed. Ultimately, the heavyweight ASW torpedo program was a failure, leaving the lightweight Mk 46 as the only shipboard torpedo.

The development of better sonars provided greater detection changes, and this required ASW weapons with increased stand-off ranges. The first

SUMNER AND GEARING MODERNIZATIONS

1. Sumner-class FRAM II unit in 1972. The first extensive modernization of Sumner-class units was the FRAM II program beginning in 1960. In addition to the internal refurbishment, the new ships emerged with a new appearance as evinced in this profile. The modernization retained all three 5in/38 twin mounts, but the 3in/50 mounts were removed. The new ASW suite can be readily seen and included the addition of a DASH flight deck and hangar, two fixed Mk 25 torpedo tubes and two triple Mk 32 launchers (all located between the two stacks), and a VDS on the fantail. The SQS-4 sonar was retained. The ships received a tripod mast for the SPS-29 air search radar and the SPS-10 surface search radar. Note the ECM equipment placed above the DASH hangar. This view also shows the new caps on the two stacks which became an identifying feature of destroyers that underwent FRAM work. This view shows *Buck* in 1962 after it completed its FRAM II work. The destroyer made six deployments to Vietnam in this configuration.

2. A Gearing-class DDE. A small number of Gearings received a minor ASW upgrade early in the Cold War and were reclassified as DDEs. These included *Lloyd Thomas,* shown here in 1949. This austere modernization included the replacement of the Number 2 5in/38 mount with a Mk 15 trainable Hedgehog launcher. Improved sonar and ECM equipment was also part of the modernization, and HF/DF gear was added on a stub mainmast. Otherwise, the ship retained its World War II appearance, including a full 20mm and 40mm battery and a quintuple torpedo bank.

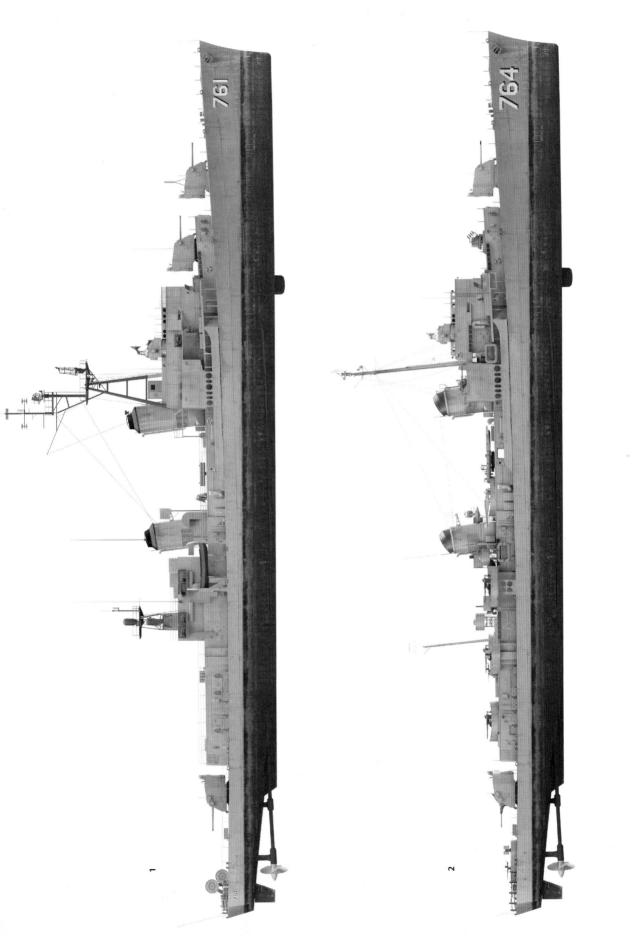

1

2

was the rocket-assisted torpedo (RAT) dating from 1953. This was a lightweight homing torpedo on a rocket with a range of 5,000yds. Even with its homing torpedo payload it was too inaccurate. The RAT program was canceled in 1957 but lessons were used to develop the successful ASROC. Development began in 1955 with a ballistic rocket designed to deliver a homing torpedo out to about 10,000yds. The rocket was fired from an eight-cell box that became ubiquitous aboard USN Cold War destroyers. ASROC's payload was the Mk 46 homing torpedo, but a 1-kiloton nuclear warhead version was deployed between 1961 and 1989.

Even greater stand-off ranges could be achieved if destroyers could carry an aerial platform. The first attempt to deploy such a capability began in 1957 with a program known as DASH. The concept of developing a drone helicopter seemed sound but proved beyond the technology of the day. To be effective, the helicopter had to be able to be airborne with its homing torpedo within 30 seconds, possess an endurance of 25 minutes,

Norfolk fires an ASROC during evaluation tests in about 1960. ASROC was one of several new pieces of equipment tested aboard *Norfolk* and it remained in service throughout the Cold War.

and required the accuracy to deliver its torpedo out to 10,000yds. The program encountered immediate problems – it was unreliable, lacked a quick reaction capability, and could not take-off with its payload under some weather conditions. In expectation of the helicopters being deployed, many Cold War destroyers were modified to operate them. This forced the USN to persist with efforts to improve DASH, but the reliability problems were never overcome. Of 746 drones built, over half were lost at sea. Program funding was stopped in 1968.

USN COLD WAR DESTROYER SENSORS

Radars

The standard early Cold War destroyer radar fit for the Fletcher, Sumner, and Gearing classes was the SPS-6 air search radar and the SPS-10 surface search radar. These replaced the SC-2 or SR air search radars and SG surface search radars. A heavier tripod mast was required to accommodate the new radars. The SPS-6A was the first postwar air search radar. It was replaced by the long-wave SPS-29 beginning in 1958. The SPS-37 was basically a pulse-compression version of the SPS-29 that used the same antennas. Only a few were fitted on Sumner–Gearing class ships during FRAM work, but it served as the primary air search radar on the Forrest Sherman class. The improved SPS-40 radar was deployed primarily on DDGs, but selected Sumners and Gearings also received it.

Height-finding radars were essential for fighter control. These were carried by the Gearing-class DDRs and the larger destroyers. The World War II-era SP was replaced by the SX in the late 1940s. Later height finders consisted of the SPS-8 and SPS-30. These were too heavy to mount on a tripod mast so were placed on the aft deckhouse.

Principal USN destroyer Cold War radars		
Radar	Purpose	Maximum range
SPS-6A/B/C	Air search	70–140nm (against large targets)
SPS-8A/B	Height-finding	72nm (actual)
SPS-10	Surface search	8nm (against a periscope-sized target)
SPS-29/37	Air search	240–270nm (theoretical)
SPS-30	Height-finding	240nm
SPS-40	Air search	200+nm

ASW sensors

ASW operations are difficult because detecting submarines is such a challenging problem. To detect submarines, all USN Cold War destroyers carried sonar. Sonar performance is affected by many factors including power, beam shape, and inclination, and a number of environmental factors that affect the speed of sound propagation underwater such as interference from the water rushing along the ship's hull (which meant that at high speeds the sonar was worthless), water temperature, salinity, and pressure (depth). Predicting the effect of environmental factors is vital to successful sonar employment.

The factors affecting sonar performance severely limited the performance of USN Cold War destroyer sonars. The standard World War II sonar was the hull-mounted QCA with a range of less than one nautical mile. The first scanning sonar (able to sweep 360 degrees) was the QHB introduced in 1946. It used lower frequencies that offered better acoustic performance. Detection ranges were still short – 2,000yds was considered excellent. The QHB was replaced by the SQS-11 or SQS-11A.

The SQS-4 entered service in the 1950s and represented a significant improvement. It was much more powerful and operated at a much lower frequency. The SQS-4 was placed in a dome under the destroyer's keel and required much more space and significant weight compensation. Placement of the new sonar in this position proved to be a problem since it was still affected by water streaming along the hull. The SQS-4 had a potential detection range out to 15,000yds but depending on environmental conditions sometimes held contacts at longer distances. Its effective range was generally about 8,000yds making the SQS-4 the first USN sonar with the potential to generate contacts at longer ranges than the ASW weapons of the day. The standard FRAM sonar was the SQS-23. It was far larger than the SQS-4 and operated at a lower frequency, giving it an effective range of 12,000yds.

VDS was developed in the 1950s to mitigate the environmental factors that degraded sonar performance. By placing the sonar on a cable and towing it behind the ship, the sonar could be lowered to a desired depth and distance astern to minimize ship's self-noise and turbulence caused by water rushing along the ship's hull and by its wake. Performance could also be improved if the sonar was placed below an otherwise impenetrable layer of water at a different temperature. The earliest VDS system placed on destroyers was the SQA-10. It used either the SQS-31

Mitscher-class ship *Willis A. Lee* photographed in drydock after installation of the prototype SQS-26 in 1966. The advanced SQS-26 was too large to be fitted to any early Cold War destroyers except the Mitscher class. It is placed on the bow in a rubber dome to increase performance.

or -32 sonar which were modified versions of the SQS-4. Early VDS was very unreliable. The cables were very susceptible to damage when they were towed. This prompted a move to more reliable and effective passive towed arrays on ASW ships.

COLD WAR GUN DESTROYERS AT WAR AND IN PEACE

Given the space available, it is obviously impossible to provide any detailed summary of the Cold War service of the many destroyers covered in this book. During the period of the Cold War up until 1975, the USN was involved in the Korean and Vietnam Wars and in a number of campaigns and expeditions. Ships were awarded battle stars (BS) for combat duty off Korea or Vietnam. There were multiple award periods for these conflicts (for example, ten for Korea), so a single ship could be awarded multiple battle stars for the same conflict. Involvement in other (usually) non-combat campaigns was recognized with campaign ribbons (CR). CRs were awarded for a wide number of peacetime operations with the primary ones being the Taiwan Strait in 1958 to protect Taiwan from a possible Chinese invasion, operations in support of the Taiwan-held islands of Quemoy and Matsu off the Chinese coast from 1959 to 1963, operations during tensions with Cuba in 1961–62, the Cuban Missile Crisis in late 1962, periods of tension off Korea in 1968–70, and interventions in Lebanon during 1958 and the Dominican Republic in 1965. Units involved in operations in the Indian Ocean or off the coast of Iran in the early 1980s also earned CRs. USN gun destroyers were present at all these hot spots. In addition, they were active all over the world during the Cold War as the USN protected American interests with a persistent naval presence.

Because of its World War II fame, the Fletcher class is not usually thought of as a Cold War warrior, but it played a prominent role in USN operations through the 1950s and into the 1960s. Fletcher-class destroyers were active throughout the Korean War (1950–53), earning a total of some 170 BSs. At least three Fletchers were damaged by Communist shore batteries during these operations. Fletchers earned some 53 CRs for operations near Quemoy–Matsu and 33 for operations in the Taiwan Strait. Tensions off Korea brought Fletchers another 11 CRs. The class was active off Cuba earning 21 CRs during tensions in 1961–62 and another ten for the Cuban Missile Crisis. Ten Fletchers took part in operations off Lebanon and one off the Dominican Republic. During the Vietnam War, Fletchers continued to give stalwart service with at least 120 deployments, many of which earned BSs.

Fletcher-class destroyer *Ingersoll* under fire from North Vietnamese shore batteries in March 1967. It was a rearmed Fletcher as evinced by the presence of only four 5in/38 mounts. Fletchers served in the Korean and Vietnam wars; *Ingersoll* made six Vietnam deployments and received three battle stars.

The history of USS *Cogswell* (DD 651)

USS *Cogswell* (DD 651) enjoyed a typical Fletcher-class career. After earning nine BSs during the Pacific War, it was decommissioned in 1946. It returned to service in 1951 in the middle of the Korean War. Assigned to the Atlantic Fleet, it conducted cruises in Northern Europe and the Mediterranean until being assigned to the Pacific Fleet in 1954. From 1955 through 1960, it conducted annual deployments to the Far East and gained a CR for Taiwan Strait operations in 1958. From 1960 until 1968 when it was decommissioned, *Cogswell* conducted another six deployments to the Western Pacific including five off Vietnam. After leaving USN service, *Cogswell* was handed over to the Turkish Navy where it served until 1980.

Cogswell underway showing the configuration of a rearmed Fletcher-class destroyer. Three 3in/50 mounts have replaced the ineffective 40mm and 20mm guns. Only four 5in/38 mounts remain. Note the addition of two Hedgehog launchers forward – this was a universal ASW upgrade for USN destroyers in the early 1950s because of its low cost. A new tripod mast is fitted with the usual SPS-6 and SPS-10 fit.

Sumner-class destroyers were also very active during the Cold War. Most saw action off either Korea or Vietnam, and many saw action in both conflicts. Ten Sumners were damaged off Korea and two off Vietnam. The most famous Sumner-class unit is *Maddox* which was involved in the Gulf of Tonkin incident in August 1964. Another famous Sumner-class ship, but for the wrong reason, was *Frank E. Evans* which was cut in two by the Australian carrier *Melbourne* in the South China Sea on June 2, 1969. Seventy-four men were killed. Sumner-class destroyers earned 157 BSs for operations off Korea and made some 121 deployments off Vietnam with many resulting in BSs. They were engaged all over the world with 15 conducting Quemoy–Matsu operations, ten recording operations in the Taiwan Strait, 27 active off Korea during times of heightened tensions, and 27 conducting operations off Cuba. Twenty-two Sumners took part in the Cuban Missile Crisis, two were active off Lebanon, and four off the Dominican Republic. One received a CR in support of operations in Laos in 1970 and one for operations in the Persian Gulf in 1961. Sumners served into the 1980s and one ship earned a CR in support of operations in the Indian Ocean in 1980.

By far the most active gun destroyers of the Cold War were the Gearing class. Combat operations were extensive, and Gearings earned 217 BSs off Korea and made some 375 Vietnam deployments. Three ships were damaged in combat operations off Korea and two off Vietnam. *Higbee* was the only USN destroyer damaged by enemy air attack during the Cold War when a North Vietnamese MiG planted a bomb on its aft 5in/38 mount in April 1972. *Warrington* hit an American

Essex-class carrier *Wasp* was the centerpiece of Anti-submarine Task Group Bravo during its Mediterranean Sea deployment in 1961. All of its escorts are Gearing-class DDEs. Aircraft in this photo opportunity include ten S2F ASW aircraft and two AD-5W early-warning aircraft. Two HSS-1 helicopters are flying just above the formation. This was the USN's envisioned use for Gearing-class destroyers during the period, functioning as part of an ASW hunter-killer group.

mine in 1972 off North Vietnam and was declared a constructive total loss. Some ships completed an enormous number of combat deployments during their careers, with three ships totaling 20 or more.

Traditional tension areas required considerable attention by the Gearings. These ships made eight Taiwan Strait deployments, 66 off Quemoy–Matsu, and 65 to Korean waters during tension periods. Thirty-five Gearings participated in quarantine operations during the Cuban Missile Crisis and 34 were active during the period of Cuban tensions. Gearings supported intervention operations in Lebanon (20 ships) and the Dominican Republic (17 ships). Four ships were involved in the evacuation from South Vietnam in 1975 and one was involved in operations to rescue the American merchant ship *Mayaquez*. Gearing-class CRs were also tied to operations in Antarctica in 1946–47 (two), and in support of UN operations in the Congo in 1961 (two).

The 18-ship Forrest Sherman class also earned recognition during the Cold War. Its ships missed the Korean War but made 63 Vietnam deployments. *Turner Joy* gained notoriety for its involvement in the Gulf of Tonkin incident. The CRs earned by these ships demonstrated the scope of their operations: four ships were involved in the 1958 Lebanon intervention, eight in the Cuban Missile Crisis, three in the Dominican Republic intervention, and one in operations in the Taiwan Strait. Forrest Shermans were active in the tension areas of Cuba (five ships), Quemoy–Matsu (ten ships), and Korea (four ships). Since the class served into the 1980s, it was also involved in other Cold War operations including the 1975 evacuation of South Vietnam and Cambodia (three ships), operations in the Indian Ocean 1978–81 (11 different deployments), and the American 1982–83 intervention in Lebanon (two ships).

The four Mitscher-class units earned a total of four BSs, all for Vietnam, and made five deployments to other crisis areas. *Norfolk* participated in the Cuban Missile Crisis.

THE DESTROYER CLASSES

The Fletcher class

The successful Fletcher class featured high speed (35kt), good endurance (4,900nm at 12kt), a heavy torpedo battery of ten tubes, and a main gun battery of five 5in guns in single mounts. By the end of World War II, the secondary battery of these ships varied, but many ships had sacrificed one bank of torpedoes for an enhanced antiaircraft battery of 12 40mm guns and 12 20mm guns. All ships retained their original five 5in guns.

By 1950, only five Fletchers remained active in the Naval Reserve. In the fiscal year (FY) 49–50 programs, 18 were modified into DDEs. Under the FY 52 program, 40 more were rearmed with the new 3in/50 gun. Two more were scheduled to receive this work in FY 52 and 40 more in FY 53, but none of this work was carried out. Another 42 ships were recommissioned but were not modernized.

The SCB 74A modernization replaced the two quad 40mm mounts abeam the second stack with twin 3in/50 mounts. Another 3in/50 twin mount replaced the Number 3 gun house. The two original quintuple torpedo mounts were removed. The two twin 40mm mounts forward of the bridge were replaced by fixed Hedgehog launchers. Launching and stowage facilities were provided for three Mk 32 homing torpedoes. Depth charge facilities were decreased to four projectors and one rack on the stern.

The old pole mast was replaced by a heavier tripod mast to take the new radars – the SPS-6 for air search and the SPS-10 for surface search. New ECM equipment, a new CIC, and a new QHB sonar were also fitted. Some units had their bridge enclosed. A larger rudder was fitted to improve steering. Along with the weapons upgrades, habitability was enhanced with the goal of giving every enlisted man a bunk and a locker for his belongings.

These ships later received a Mk 32 triple torpedo launcher and the SQS-4 sonar was later added at the expense of the four depth charge projectors.

The Fletcher DDE conversion was more extensive. Three 5in/38 mounts, all 40mm guns, and both torpedo mounts were removed. A Weapon Alpha, Mk 15 trainable Hedgehog, and four fixed torpedo tubes were added for ASW. Two twin 3in/50 and four twin 20mm mounts constituted the secondary battery. These DDEs were little modified thereafter. Three received a FRAM II modernization which added a DASH flight deck and hangar and new ECM equipment. Late in their careers, the FRAM units carried a fit

Fletcher-class *Bache* photographed underway on July 21, 1964 still in the DDE configuration that it received in the early 1950s. Note the single 5in/38 mount forward and the Weapon Alpha. Other ASW weapons include the Hedgehog launchers abreast the bridge and the Mk 32 torpedo tubes fitted between the stacks. The ship's primary electronics are also visible including a SPS-6 and SPS-10 on the foremast, a Mk 37 director with a Mk 25 radar above the bridge, and a Mk 56 director aft.

of two 5in/38 and two 3in/50 mounts, one Weapon Alpha, two Hedgehog launchers, two fixed torpedo tubes, two Mk 32 launchers, and an SQS-4 sonar. At a cost of $6.8 million, this conversion was too expensive to carry out on all Fletchers as originally intended. Such an investment was unwise in an era in which ASW technology was rapidly changing. With the exception of three units, FRAM funding was not used for Fletcher-class ships. Fifteen more Fletchers were slated to receive FRAM work in 1961, but funding was shifted to Gearing-class ships.

The other ships that returned to service received a lighter modernization that resembled the 1945 program to defend against kamikaze attack. The original five 5in guns, all in single mounts, were retained, as was one of the quintuple torpedo mounts. If they had not already received two 40mm quad mounts amidships in place of one of the torpedo mounts, these were fitted. The forward twin 40mm mounts were replaced by fixed Hedgehogs.

This austere modernization also included some electronics improvements. The Mk 37 fire control director received the Mk 25 radar to replace the Mk 12/22 sets. The SG surface search radar was replaced by the SU, but the SC-2 air search radar was retained. Some ships were later given new radars (SPS-6 and SPS-10) and a heavier tripod mast. All ships received larger rudders to improve handling. In this condition, the Fletchers were seriously overweight.

In 1958, 61 Fletchers were still active. Of these, 23 had the original five-gun configuration. In 1965, only 16 were active with only two still in the original five-gun configuration. As the ships reached the end of their active careers, some of the ineffective weapons were removed. The 40mm and 3in/50 mounts were removed and those ships with torpedo mounts lost them. In 1971, only two Fletchers remained and these were used for reserve training. One of these was *Shields* which had been in continuous service since its commissioning in 1945 until being decommissioned in 1972.

Fletcher-class Cold War units				
Ship	Recommissioned	Modernization	Decommissioned	Fate
Fletcher (DD 445)	October 4, 1949	DDE 1949	August 1, 1969	Scrapped 1972
Radford (DD 446)	October 18, 1949	DDE 1949; FRAM II 1960	November 10, 1969	Scrapped 1970
Jenkins (DD 447)	November 3, 1951	DDE 1951; FRAM II 1961	July 2, 1969	Scrapped 1971
Nicholas (DD 449)	February 20, 1951	DDE 1949; FRAM II 1960	January 30, 1970	Scrapped 1970
O'Bannon (DD 450)	February 20, 1951	DDE 1949	January 30, 1970	Scrapped 1970
Saufley (DD 465)	December 16, 1949	DDE 1949	January 29, 1965	Sunk as target 1968
Waller (DD 466)	July 6, 1950	DDE 1950	July 15, 1969	Sunk as target 1970
Taylor (DD 468)	December 4, 1951	DDE 1951	June 3, 1969	Transferred to Italy 1969
Bache (DD 470)	October 2, 1951	DDE 1951	N/A	Wrecked in storm February 6, 1968
Beale (DD 471)	November 2, 1951	DDE 1951	October 1, 1968	Sunk as target 1969
Philip (DD 498)	July 1, 1950	DDE 1950	September 30, 1968	Sold for scrap 1971; foundered
Renshaw (DD 499)	June 3, 1950	DDE 1950	February 14, 1969	Scrapped 1970
Conway (DD 507)	November 8, 1950	DDE 1949	November 15, 1969	Sunk as target 1970
Cony (DD 508)	November 18, 1949	DDE 1949	July 2, 1969	Sunk as target 1970
Eaton (DD 510)	December 12, 1951	DDE 1951	July 2, 1969	Sunk as target 1970
Walker (DD 517)	September 16, 1950	DDE 1949	July 2, 1969	Transferred to Italy
Daly (DD 519)	July 7, 1951	Rearmed	May 2, 1960	Scrapped 1976

Fletcher-class Cold War units

Ship	Recommissioned	Modernization	Decommissioned	Fate
Isherwood (DD 520)	April 6, 1951	Rearmed	September 11, 1961	Transferred to Peru 1961
Kimberly (DD 521)	February 8, 1951	None	January 16, 1954	Transferred to Taiwan 1967
Ammen (DD 527)	April 6, 1951	Rearmed	September 15, 1960	Scrapped 1961
Mullaney (DD 528)	March 9, 1951	Rearmed	October 6, 1971	Transferred to Taiwan
Trathen (DD 530)	August 2, 1951	Rearmed	May 11, 1965	Scrapped 1973
Hazelwood (DD 531)	September 13, 1951	Test ship for DASH	March 19, 1965	Scrapped 1976
Heermann (DD 532)	September 13, 1951	Rearmed	December 20, 1957	Transferred to Argentina 1961
McCord (DD 534)	August 2, 1951	None	June 9, 1954	Scrapped 1974
Miller (DD 535)	May 20, 1951	Rearmed	June 30, 1964	Scrapped 1975
Owen (DD 536)	August 18, 1951	None	May 27, 1958	Scrapped 1973
The Sullivans (DD 537)	July 7, 1951	Rearmed	January 7, 1965	Museum ship Buffalo, New York
Stephen Potter (DD 538)	March 30, 1951	None	April 21, 1958	Scrapped 1973
Tingey (DD 539)	January 28, 1951	None	November 30, 1963	Sunk as target 1966
Twining (DD 540)	June 11, 1950	None	July 1, 1971	Transferred to Taiwan 1971
Yarnell (DD 541)	March 1, 1951	None	September 30, 1958	Transferred to Taiwan 1968
Boyd (DD 544)	November 25, 1950	Rearmed	October 1, 1969	Transferred to Turkey
Bradford (DD 545)	October 28, 1950	None	September 28, 1962	Transferred to Greece 1962
Brown (DD 546)	October 28, 1950	None	October 18, 1962	Transferred to Greece 1962
Cowell (DD 547)	September 22, 1951	Rearmed	August 17, 1971	Transferred to Argentina 1971
Hailey (DD 556)	April 28, 1951	Rearmed	November 3, 1960	Transferred to Brazil 1961
Laws (DD 558)	November 3, 1951	None	March 30, 1964	Scrapped 1973
Prichett (DD 561)	August 18, 1951	Rearmed	January 10, 1970	Transferred to Italy 1970
Robinson (DD 562)	August 4, 1951	None	June 1, 1964	Sunk as target 1982
Ross (DD 563)	October 28, 1951	None	November 6, 1959	Sunk as target 1975
Rowe (DD 564)	October 6, 1951	Rearmed	November 6, 1959	Sunk as target 1978
Smalley (DD 565)	July 4, 1951	None	September 30, 1957	Scrapped 1966
Stoddard (DD 566)	March 10, 1951	Rearmed	September 26, 1969	Sunk 1997
Watts (DD 567)	July 7, 1951	None	September 26, 1969	Scrapped 1975
Wren (DD 568)	September 8, 1951	None	December 1963	Scrapped 1975
Murray (DD 576)	November 16, 1951	DDE	May 1966	Scrapped 1966
Sproston (DD 577)	September 16, 1950	DDE	September 30, 1968	Scrapped 1971
Shields (DD 596)	July 16, 1950	None	July 1, 1972	Transferred to Brazil 1972
Abbot (DD 629)	February 27, 1951	Rearmed	March 26, 1965	Scrapped 1975
Braine (DD 630)	April 7, 1951	Rearmed	August 17, 1971	Transferred to Argentina 1971
Erben (DD 631)	May 20, 1951	None	June 27, 1958	Transferred to South Korea 1963
Hale (DD 642)	March 25, 1951	Rearmed	July 30, 1960	Transferred to Colombia 1961
Sigourney (DD 643)	September 8, 1951	None	May 1, 1960	Scrapped 1975
Strembel (DD 644)	November 10, 1951	Rearmed	May 27, 1958	Transferred to Argentina 1961
Caperton (DD 650)	April 10, 1951	Rearmed	April 27, 1960	Sunk as target
Cogswell (DD 651)	January 8, 1951	Rearmed	October 1, 1968	Transferred to Turkey 1969
Ingersoll (DD 652)	May 5, 1951	Rearmed	January 20, 1970	Sunk as target 1974
Knapp (DD 653)	May 4, 1951	None	March 4, 1957	Scrapped 1973
Bearss (DD 654)	September 8, 1951	None	December 30, 1963	Scrapped 1976
John Hood (DD 655)	August 4, 1951	Rearmed	1964	Scrapped 1976
Van Valkenburgh (DD 656)	March 9, 1951	None	February 26, 1954	Transferred to Turkey 1967
Charles J. Badger (DD 657)	September 11, 1951	None	December 20, 1957	Transferred to Chile for parts 1974
Colahan (DD 658)	December 17, 1950	None	August 1, 1966	Sunk as target 1966

Fletcher-class Cold War units

Ship	Recommissioned	Modernization	Decommissioned	Fate
Dashiell (DD 659)	May 4, 1951	Rearmed	April 29, 1960	Scrapped 1975
Kidd (DD 661)	March 29, 1951	None	June 19, 1964	Museum ship, Baton Rouge, Louisiana
Black (DD 666)	July 19, 1951	Rearmed	September 21, 1969	Scrapped 1971
Chauncey (DD 667)	July 19, 1950	None	May 14, 1954	Scrapped 1974
Clarence K. Bronson (DD 668)	June 8, 1951	None	June 29, 1960	Transferred to Turkey 1967
Cotten (DD 669)	July 4, 1951	Rearmed	May 2, 1960	Scrapped 1975
Dortch (DD 670)	May 5, 1951	Rearmed	December 13, 1957	Transferred to Argentina 1961
Gatling (DD 671)	June 5, 1951	None	May 2, 1960	Scrapped 1977
Healy (DD 672)	August 4, 1951	None	March 11, 1958	Scrapped 1976
Hickox (DD 673)	May 20, 1951	None	December 20, 1957	Transferred to South Korea 1968
Hunt (DD 674)	November 1, 1951	Rearmed	December 30, 1963	Scrapped 1975
Lewis Hancock (DD 675)	May 20, 1951	None	December 18, 1957	Transferred to Brazil 1967
Marshall (DD 676)	April 28, 1951	None	July 19, 1969	Scrapped 1970
McDermut (DD 677)	December 30, 1950	Rearmed	December 16, 1963	Scrapped 1966
McGowan (DD 678)	July 7, 1951	Rearmed	November 30, 1960	Transferred to Spain
McNair (DD 679)	July 7, 1951	Rearmed	December 30, 1963	Scrapped 1976
Melvin (DD 680)	February 27, 1951	None	January 13, 1954	Scrapped 1975
Hopewell (DD 681)	March 29, 1951	Rearmed	January 2, 1970	Sunk as target 1972
Porterfield (DD 682)	April 28, 1951	None	November 7, 1969	Sunk as target 1982
Stockham (DD 683)	November 15, 1951	None	September 2, 1957	Sunk as target 1977
Wedderburn (DD 684)	November 22, 1950	None	October 1, 1969	Scrapped 1972
Picking (DD 685)	January 27, 1951	Prototype for rearmed ships	September 6, 1969	Sunk as target 1997
Halsey Powell (DD 686)	April 28, 1951	None	April 27, 1968	Transferred to South Korea
Uhlmann (DD 687)	May 24, 1950	Rearmed	July 15, 1972	Scrapped 1974
Remey (DD 688)	November 15, 1951	None	December 30, 1963	Scrapped 1975
Wadleigh (DD 689)	October 4, 1951	Rearmed	June 28, 1962	Transferred to Chile 1962
Cassin Young (DD 793)	September 9, 1951	Rearmed	April 29, 1960	Museum ship Boston, Massachusetts
Irwin (DD 794)	February 27, 1951	Rearmed	January 10, 1958	Transferred to Brazil 1968
Preston (DD 795)	January 27, 1951	Rearmed	November 15, 1969	Transferred to Turkey 1969
Benham (DD 796)	March 25, 1951	Rearmed	December 15, 1960	Transferred to Peru 1960
Cushing (DD 797)	August 18, 1951	None	November 8, 1960	Transferredto Brazil 1961
Monssen (DD 798)	November 1, 1951	None	December 11, 1957	Scrapped 1963
Jarvis (DD 799)	February 9, 1951	Rearmed	October 24, 1960	Transferred to Spain 1960
Porter (DD 800)	February 10, 1951	None	August 10, 1953	Scrapped 1974
Gregory (DD 802)	April 28, 1951	None	February 1, 1964	Expended as target 1971
Rooks (DD 804)	May 20, 1951	Rearmed	July 26, 1962	Transferred to Chile 1962

In addition to the units that served in the USN during the Cold War, many others were turned over to foreign navies. Thirteen were given the rearmament modification before being transferred; six to West Germany, four to Greece, two to Japan, and one to Spain. In addition to these transfers and the ones indicated in the table above, others were pulled from reserve and gifted to foreign navies. These included two for Brazil, one for Mexico, and two more for Spain. This left 41 units that remained in reserve and saw no further service after World War II.

Fletcher-class specifications (as built)	
Displacement	2,050 tons standard; 3,040 tons full load
Dimensions	Length 377ft; beam 40ft; draft 18ft
Machinery	2 shafts making 60,000shp
Performance	37kt; 6,500nm at 15kt
Crew	315 after modernization

Ault pictured in the mid-1950s showing the configuration of a rearmed Sumner-class destroyer. Two 3in/50 mounts have been fitted aft of the second stack replacing the original 40mm guns. Note the addition of the Hedgehogs abreast the bridge and the new tripod mast.

Sumner class

As completed, the Sumners were heavily armed with three twin 5in/38 mounts, 12 40mm guns in twin and quadruple mounts, 11 20mm single mounts, and two quintuple torpedo mounts. Fifty-eight ships were built to the original destroyer design. Of these, three were lost in the war and another was damaged so badly by kamikazes that it was not repaired. Another was scrapped shortly after the war. Almost all of the remaining units were kept in commission after the war. The few that weren't were brought back into commission at the start of the Korean War. A total of 53 Sumner-class destroyers were active during the Cold War.

These ships required warfare and habitability improvements to remain useful. The first modernization was a rearmament program conducted in FY 52. Forty Sumners were given this upgrade. The last 13 units were scheduled to receive this work as part of the FY 53 program, but inadequate funding precluded this from being done. This initial modernization replaced the 40mm Bofors guns with six 3in/50 guns in two twin and two single mounts. The 13 units not upgraded retained their 40mm battery through the 1950s. The original rearmament program also removed the 20mm guns and added fixed Hedgehog launchers abeam the bridge. The depth charge projectors aft were also removed and launching racks for homing torpedoes added. Habitability was also enhanced as part of the modernization. Since ASW became the primary focus of these ships, constant efforts were made to upgrade their ASW capabilities. However, funding issues kept these improvements to a minimum until the FRAM II program was approved. Initial ASW upgrades included the addition of two Hedgehog launchers forward. The QHB sonar was replaced by SQS-11 or 11A, and in the mid-50s, the class received the much more capable SQS-4.

THE GULF OF TONKIN INCIDENT

The Gulf of Tonkin incident on August 2, 1964 was a major milestone on the path to full involvement by the United States in the Vietnam War. In the summer of 1964, Seventh Fleet forces were very active off the coast of North Vietnam. These operations included intelligence collection missions in the Tonkin Gulf. *Maddox*, a Sumner-class destroyer, was conducting such a mission on August 2, 1964 when it was approached by three P-4-class torpedo boats of the North Vietnamese Navy. When the torpedo boats closed to within 10,000yds of the destroyer at high speed, *Maddox* fired warning shots with its 5in guns. This did not deter the North Vietnamese; two torpedo boats fired a single torpedo and attacked with machine guns. *Maddox* evaded the torpedoes and was hit by only a single 14.5mm machine gun round. This scene shows the destroyer firing at the P-4s. One of the three boats was hit by *Maddox*'s fire but survived.

A second incident occurred two days later with *Maddox* and a second destroyer, the Forrest Sherman-class destroyer *Turner Joy*. This action took place at night with the Americans claiming they were attacked again by North Vietnamese torpedo boats. In fact, there was no attack, but the incident prompted American retaliation and led to an expanded role in the war.

Beginning in 1960, the Sumner class underwent FRAM II modernization. It was intended that the entire class receive this modernization, but in 1961 work on 17 Sumners was canceled to provide more funding for the Gearings to receive FRAM upgrades. Sumner FRAM II work was extensive. It included all the hull and machinery work from FRAM I and combat systems upgrades. Following the completion of FRAM II work, a Sumner retained its three 5in/38 twin mounts, but all other guns were removed. ASW capabilities were significantly upgraded with the addition of a DASH flight deck and hangar, two fixed Mk 25 torpedo tubes, two triple Mk 32 launchers, and a VDS on the stern. The SQS-4 sonar was retained. The appearance of the ships changed with bridge modifications, a new radar mast mounting the SPS-29 air search radar and the SPS-10 surface search radar, and ECM equipment located around the aft stack.

Sumner-class construction

Ship	Commissioned	Modernization	Decommissioned	Fate
Allen M. Sumner (DD 692)	January 26, 1944	Rearmed; FRAM II 1961	August 15, 1973	Scrapped 1974
Moale (DD 693)	February 28, 1944	Rearmed; FRAM II 1961	July 2, 1973	Scrapped 1974
Ingraham (DD 694)	March 10, 1944	Rearmed; FRAM II 1961	June 16, 1971	Transferred to Greece 1971
English (DD 696)	May 4, 1944	Rearmed	May 15, 1970	Transferred to Taiwan 1970
Charles S. Sperry (DD 697)	May 17, 1944; recommissioned July 1, 1950	Rearmed; FRAM II 1960	December 15, 1973	Transferred to Chile 1974
Ault (DD 698)	May 31, 1944; recommissioned November 15, 1950	Rearmed; FRAM II 1962	July 16, 1973	Scrapped 1974
Waldron (DD 699)	June 8, 1944; recommissioned November 20, 1950	FRAM II 1962	October 30, 1973	Transferred to Columbia 1973
Haynsworth (DD 700)	June 22, 1944; recommissioned September 22, 1950	None	January 30, 1970	Transferred to Taiwan 1970
John W. Weeks (DD 701)	July 21, 1944; recommissioned October 24, 1950	None	August 12, 1970	Sunk as target 1970
Hank (DD 702)	August 28, 1944	Rearmed	July 1, 1972	Transferred to Argentina
Wallace L. Lind (DD 703)	September 8, 1944	Rearmed; FRAM II 1962	December 4, 1973	Transferred to South Korea
Borie (DD 704)	September 21, 1944; recommissioned September 19, 1949	Rearmed; FRAM II 1962	July 1, 1972	Transferred to Argentina
Compton (DD 705)	November 4, 1944	Rearmed	September 27, 1972	Transferred to Brazil
Gainard (DD 706)	November 23, 1944	Rearmed	February 26, 1971	Scrapped 1974
Soley (DD 707)	December 7, 1944; recommissioned January 29, 1949	Rearmed	February 13, 1970	Sunk as target 1970
Harlan R. Dickson (DD 708)	February 17, 1945	Rearmed	July 1, 1972	Scrapped 1973
Hugh Purvis (DD 709)	March 1, 1945	Rearmed; FRAM II 1960	June 15, 1972	Transferred to Turkey 1972
Barton (DD 722)	December 30, 1943; recommissioned April 11, 1949	Rearmed	October 1, 1968	Sunk as target 1969
Walke (DD 723)	January 21, 1944; recommissioned October 5, 1950	Rearmed; FRAM II 1961	November 30, 1970	Scrapped 1975
Laffey (DD 724)	February 8, 1944; recommissioned January 26, 1951	Rearmed; FRAM II 1962	March 29, 1975	Museum ship in Charleston, South Carolina
O'Brien (DD 725)	March 10, 1944; recommissioned October 5, 1950	Rearmed; FRAM II 1961	February 18, 1972	Sunk as target 1972
De Haven (DD 727)	March 31, 1944	Rearmed; FRAM II 1960	December 3, 1973	Transferred to South Korea 1973
Mansfield (DD 728)	April 14, 1944	Rearmed; FRAM II 1960	February 1, 1974	Transferred to Argentina for parts 1974

Sumner-class construction

Ship	Commissioned	Modernization	Decommissioned	Fate
Lyman K. Swenson (DD 729)	May 2, 1944	Rearmed; FRAM II 1961	February 12, 1971	Scrapped 1974
Collett (DD 730)	May 16, 1944	FRAM II 1960	December 18, 1970	Transferred to Argentina 1974
Maddox (DD 731)	June 2, 1944	Rearmed	July 1, 1972	Transferred to Taiwan 1972
Hyman (DD 732)	June 16, 1944	Rearmed	November 16, 1969	Scrapped 1970
Purdy (DD 734)	July 18, 1944	None	July 2, 1973	Scrapped 1974
Blue (DD 744)	March 20, 1944; recommissioned May 14, 1949	Rearmed; FRAM II 1961	January 27, 1971	Sunk as target 1977
Brush (DD 745)	April 17, 1944	Rearmed	October 27, 1969	Transferred to Taiwan 1969
Taussig (DD 746)	May 20, 1944	Rearmed; FRAM II 1962	December 1, 1970	Transferred to Taiwan 1974
Samuel N. Moore (DD 747)	June 24, 1944	None	October 24, 1969	Transferred to Taiwan 1969
Harry E. Hubbard (DD 748)	July 22, 1944; recommissioned May 14, 1949	Rearmed	October 17, 1969	Scrapped 1970
Alfred A. Cunningham (DD 752)	November 23, 1944; recommissioned October 5, 1950	Rearmed; FRAM II 1961	February 24, 1971	Sunk as target 1979
John R. Pierce (DD 753)	December 30, 1944	Rearmed	July 2, 1973	Scrapped 1974
Frank E. Evans (DD 754)	February 3, 1945; recommissioned September 15, 1950	Rearmed; FRAM II 1961	N/A	Collided with Australian carrier Melbourne June 2, 1969
John A. Bole (DD 755)	March 3, 1945	Rearmed; FRAM II 1962	February 1, 1974	Transferred to Taiwan for parts 1974
Beatty (DD 756)	March 31, 1945	None	July 14, 1972	Transferred to Venezuela 1972
Putnam (DD 757)	October 12, 1944; recommissioned October 23, 1950	Rearmed; FRAM II 1962	August 6, 1973	Scrapped 1974
Strong (DD 758)	March 8, 1945; recommissioned May 14, 1949	Rearmed; FRAM II 1962	September 30, 1973	Transferred to Brazil 1973
Lofberg (DD 759)	April 26, 1945	FRAM II 1962	January 15, 1971	Transferred to Taiwan for parts 1974
John W. Thomason (DD 760)	October 11, 1945	FRAM II 1960	December 8, 1970	Transferred to Taiwan 1970
Buck (DD 761)	June 28, 1946	FRAM II 1962	July 16, 1973	Transferred to Brazil
Henley (DD 762)	October 8, 1946; recommissioned September 23, 1950	Rearmed	July 1, 1973	Scrapped 1974
Lowry (DD 770)	July 23, 1944; recommissioned December 27, 1950	Rearmed; FRAM II 1960	October 29, 1973	Transferred to Brazil
Willard Keith (DD 775)	December 27, 1944	Rearmed	July 1, 1972	Transferred to Colombia 1972
James C. Owens (DD 776)	February 17, 1945; recommissioned September 20, 1950	Rearmed; FRAM II 1962	July 15, 1973	Transferred to Brazil
Zellars (DD 777)	October 25, 1944	Rearmed; FRAM II 1960	March 19, 1971	Transferred to Iran 1973
Massey (DD 778)	November 24, 1944	FRAM II 1960	September 17, 1973	Scrapped 1974
Douglas H. Fox (DD 779)	December 26, 1944; recommissioned November 15, 1950	Rearmed; FRAM II 1962	December 15, 1973	Transferred to Chile 1974
Stormes (DD 780)	January 27, 1945; recommissioned October 23, 1950	Rearmed; FRAM II 1961	December 5, 1970	Transferred to Iran 1972
Robert K. Huntington (DD 781)	March 3, 1945	FRAM II 1960	October 13, 1973	Transferred to Venezuela
Bristol (DD 857)	March 17, 1945	None	November 21, 1969	Transferred to Taiwan 1969

In addition, another 12 units were built as minelayers and given the classification DMS. They saw no action during World War II in their intended role. By 1950, only four remained active. By the end of the Korean War, only two remained. They were finally retired in 1958.

Sumner-class specifications (as built)	
Displacement	2,200 tons standard; 3,315 tons full load
Dimensions	Length 376ft, 6in; beam 40ft, 10in; draft 13ft (design)
Machinery	2 shafts making 60,000shp
Performance	36.5kt (design); 6,500nm at 15kt
Crew	345

Gearing class

By adding 14ft to the hull of a Sumner-class unit, the Gearing class was created. The added length resulted in increased bunkerage and therefore greater endurance. Other than that, there were no changes. The Gearing was nothing more than a production variant of the Sumner class. A total of 93 were completed to the original destroyer design. Nine more were delivered incomplete. Of these, four were completed in 1949 as prototypes for new types of ASW escorts and *Timmerman* was completed in 1952 to test a new propulsion system.

Beginning in FY 51, the Gearings received their first modernizations. This was a rearmament that replaced the 40mm and 20mm guns with six 3in/50 guns in two twin mounts abaft the second stack and two single 5in/50 mounts near the bridge. In FY 52, 33 Gearings received this upgrade, as did all 36 DDR Gearings. FY 53 included plans to rearm the last 11 Gearings, but this work was not accomplished. As the focus of the Gearings increasingly became ASW, all ships received minor ASW upgrades. Two Hedgehog launchers replaced the forward single 3in/50 guns. The QHB sonar was replaced by the SQS-11 or 11A; in the mid-1950s, these ships were fitted with the SQS-4.

Reflecting the emphasis on ASW, 15 Gearings were modified into DDEs or DDKs. *Basilone* and *Epperson* were completed as extensively modified prototype DDEs. Each carried one Weapon Alpha in place of the Number 2 5in/38 mount, two Mk 15 Hedgehogs and four fixed torpedo tubes in the new amidships deckhouse. Both also had their bridge structures extensively

modified. *Carpenter* and *Robert A. Owens* were completed as prototype DDKs and tested the Weapon Alpha and 3in/70 twin mounts planned for the ASW cruiser *Norfolk*. The other 11 ships received a much less extensive DDE conversion with a Mk 15 Hedgehog launcher replacing the Number 2 5in/38 mount. A pair of Mk 11 fixed Hedgehogs was fitted abreast the bridge.

An important Gearing variant was the DDR. In preparation for the invasion of Japan and an increased kamikaze threat, 24 Gearings were completed as DDRs. These ships lost their remaining bank of torpedoes for a tripod mast carrying the SP height-finding radar so important for fighter direction. DDRs were considered to be an essential aspect of carrier task groups, so the FY 52 program included another 12 DDR conversions. These were equipped with the latest height-finder, the SPS-8. It was too heavy to place on a mast, so was positioned on a deckhouse abaft the second stack. To compensate for the extra weight of the SPS-8, the two single 3in/50 guns forward of the bridge were removed and replaced with two Hedgehogs. The DDRs also received ASW upgrades in the form of the SQS-4 sonar, even

GEARING-CLASS FRAM I DESTROYER

The iconic USN gun destroyer of the Cold War was the Gearing FRAM I class. This is USS *Wiltsie* in 1965 during the first of its eight Vietnam deployments. It was a FRAM I Group B ship, the most numerous FRAM I conversion.

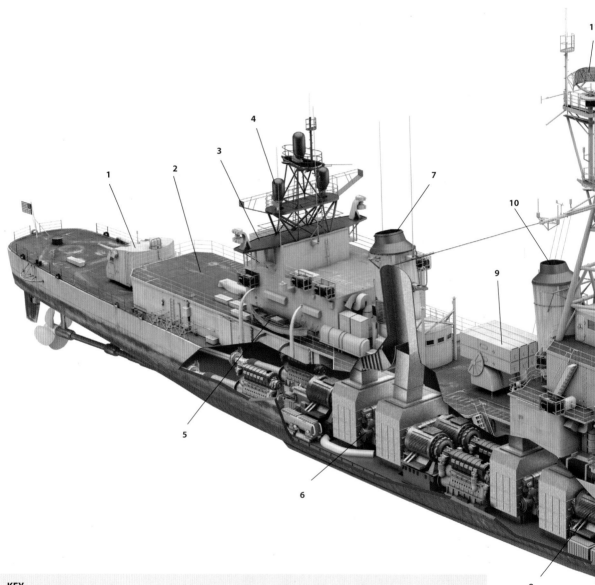

KEY

1. Aft 5in/38 mount
2. DASH flight deck
3. DASH hangar
4. Main mast with ECM gear
5. Ship's boat
6. Aft fireroom with boilers three and four
7. Aft stack with new caps
8. Forward engine room
9. ASROC launcher

10. Forward stack with new caps
11. SPS-10 surface search radar
12. SPS-29 air search radar
13. Mk 37 fire control director with Mk 25 radar
14. Navigation bridge
15. Mk 32 torpedo tubes (two mounts)
16. SQS-23 sonar
17. Shell handling room
18. Forward 5in/38 mount

12

13

14

18

15

16

17

716

716

William C. Lawe photographed in about 1983. It is a good example of a FRAM I Group B conversion. The main difference between Group A and B units is the presence of Mk 32 torpedo tubes forward of the bridge on Group B ships. All but a few Gearing FRAM I conversions assumed the Group B configuration.

though on some ships this required the loss of one or two of the twin 3in/50 mounts. By the time the FRAM program was implemented, most DDRs had reverted to ASW destroyers since there were new ships coming into service with much better capabilities than the aging Gearing DDR conversions. Six ships were retained as DDRs and were fitted with the SPS-30 height-finding radar and the SPS-29 or 40 air search radars, as well as the SQA-10 VDS.

Other Gearings performed in experimental duties. *Kraus* was reclassified as an experimental unit in 1949. It was reclassified as a DD in 1954 and later received FRAM I work. *Timmerman* was the last of the Gearings. It was completed in 1952 with a high-temperature, high-pressure steam plant that could produce 100,000shp in the same space as the 60,000shp in the other wartime destroyers. It was completed with no torpedo tubes, depth charge equipment, or Hedgehogs, but carried the standard 40mm fit. It carried the modified DDE bridge.

Gyatt became the USN's first DDG. A twin launcher for the Terrier SAM system was placed aft and the 5in mounts replaced by 3in/50 mounts. *Sarsfield* and *Witek* were used to test new weapons planned for the DDE/DDK ships. In 1947, they had their Number 2 5in/38 mount removed and replaced with the Mk 15 trainable Hedgehog and two Mk 10 or Mk 11 fixed Hedgehog launchers. They were not reclassified as DDEs. *Sarsfield* later received FRAM work, but *Witek* was one of only three Gearings that did not.

Beginning in FY 61, the Gearings began to undergo FRAM modernization. As indicated above, most Gearings received FRAM I work with its emphasis on increasing their ASW capabilities. All ships received an ASROC launcher amidships, DASH facilities, two Mk 32 torpedo launchers, an SQS-23 sonar, and a new electronics suite. Only two 5in/38 mounts were retained. On the eight Group A ships, both mounts were forward of the bridge and the Mk 32 launchers were placed aft. The placement of the torpedo tubes was unsatisfactory, so most ships were completed in the Group B configuration of one 5in/38 mount forward with the two Mk 32 launchers on the 01 level forward of the bridge; the second 5in/38 mount was placed aft.

Sixteen Gearings received FRAM II work. These included six former DDEs, four former DDRs, and six DDRs that were retained in that role. These ships looked like Sumner-class units since they retained all three 5in/38 mounts. FRAM II Gearings did not receive an ASROC launcher or DASH facilities. The former DDRs received two fixed Mk 25 torpedo tubes, while the six ships kept as DDRs were fitted with the SQS-23 and VDS, the SPS-30 radar, and Mk 32 torpedo tubes.

Of note, during the Vietnam War ten Gearings received Shrike antiradiation and Sea Chaparral IR-homing missiles to counteract threats off Vietnam.

Gearing-class construction				
Ship	Commissioned	Modernization	Decommissioned	Fate
Gearing (DD 710)	May 3, 1945	Retained 40mm guns through the 1950s; FRAM I 1962	July 1, 1973	Scrapped 1974
Eugene A. Greene (DD 711)	June 8, 1945	DDR 1952; FRAM I (Group B) 1963	August 31, 1972	Transferred to Spain 1972
Gyatt (DD 712)	July 2, 1945	Retained 40mm guns through the 1950s; DDG 1956	October 22, 1969	Sunk as target 1970
Kenneth D. Bailey (DD 713)	July 31, 1945	DDR 1953; FRAM II 1960 (kept as DDR)	April 2, 1970	Transferred to Iran for parts 1975
William D. Rush (DD 714)	September 21, 1945	DDR 1953; FRAM I (Group B) 1965	July 1, 1978	Transferred to South Korea 1978
William M. Wood (DD 715)	December 16, 1949	DDR 1953; FRAM I (Group B) 1965	December 1, 1976	Sunk as target 1983
Wiltsie (DD 716)	January 12, 1946	FRAM I (Group B) 1962	January 23, 1976	Transferred to Pakistan 1977
Theodore E. Chandler (DD 717)	March 22, 1946	FRAM I (Group B) 1962	April 1, 1975	Scrapped 1975
Hamner (DD 718)	July 12, 1946	FRAM I (Group B) 1962	October 1, 1979	Transferred to Taiwan 1980
Epperson (DD 719)	March 19, 1949	Prototype DDE 1949; FRAM I (Group B) 1964	December 1, 1975	Transferred to Pakistan 1977
Frank Knox (DD 742)	December 11, 1944	DDR 1945; FRAM II 1961 (kept as DDR)	January 30, 1971	Transferred to Greece 1971
Southerland (DD 743)	December 22, 1944	DDR 1945; FRAM I (Group B) 1964	February 23, 1981	Sunk as target 1997
William C. Lawe (DD 763)	December 18, 1946	FRAM I (Group B) 1961	October 1, 1983	Sunk as target 1999
Lloyd Thomas (DD 764)	March 21, 1947	DDE 1947; FRAM II 1961	October 12, 1972	Transferred to Taiwan
Keppler (DD 765)	May 23, 1947	DDE 1947; FRAM II 1961	July 1, 1972	Transferred to Turkey 1972
Rowan (DD 782)	March 31, 1945	Retained 40mm guns through the 1950s; FRAM I (Group B) 1964	December 18, 1975	Transferred to Taiwan 1977 but sank en route
Gurke (DD 783)	May 12, 1945	Retained 40mm guns through the 1950s; FRAM I 1964	January 20, 1976	Transferred to Greece 1977
McKean (DD 784)	June 9, 1945	DDR 1953, FRAM I (Group B) 1964	October 1, 1981	Transferred to Turkey for parts 1982
Henderson (DD 785)	August 4, 1945	Retained 40mm guns through the 1950s; FRAM I (Group B) 1962	September 30, 1980	Transferred to Pakistan 1980
Richard B. Anderson (DD 786)	October 26, 1945	FRAM I (Group A) 1961	December 20, 1975	Transferred to Taiwan 1977
James E. Kyes (DD 787)	February 8, 1946	Retained 40mm guns through the 1950s; FRAM I (Group B) 1963	March 31, 1973	Transferred to Taiwan 1973
Hollister (DD 788)	March 26, 1946	FRAM I (Group B) 1961	August 31, 1979	Transferred to Taiwan 1983
Eversole (DD 789)	July 10, 1946	FRAM I (Group B) 1963	July 11, 1973	Transferred to Turkey 1973
Shelton (DD 790)	June 21, 1946	FRAM I (Group A) 1961	March 31, 1973	Transferred to Taiwan 1973
Chevalier (DD 805)	January 9, 1945	DDR 1945; FRAM II 1962	July 1, 1972	Transferred to South Korea 1972
Higbee (DD 806)	January 27, 1945	DDR 1945; FRAM I (Group B) 1964	July 15, 1979	Sunk as target 1983
Benner (DD 807)	February 13, 1945	DDR 1945; FRAM II 1963	November 20, 1970	Scrapped 1975
Dennis J. Buckley (DD 808)	March 2, 1945	DDR 1945; FRAM I (Group B) 1964	July 2, 1973	Scrapped 1974

Gearing-class construction

Ship	Commissioned	Modernization	Decommissioned	Fate
Corry (DD 817)	February 27, 1946	DDR 1953; FRAM I (Group B) 1964	February 27, 1981	Transferred to Greece 1981
New (DD 818)	April 5, 1946	DDE 1950; FRAM I (Group B) 1963	July 1, 1976	Transferred to South Korea 1977
Holder (DD 819)	May 18, 1946	DDE 1950; FRAM I (Group B) 1963	October 1, 1976	Transferred to Ecuador 1978
Rich (DD 820)	July 3, 1946	DDE 1950; FRAM I (Group B) 1963	December 15, 1977	Scrapped 1979
Johnston (DD 821)	August 23, 1946	FRAM I (Group B) 1962	February 27, 1981	Transferred to Taiwan 1981
Robert H. McCard (DD 822)	October 26, 1946	FRAM I (Group B) 1962	June 5, 1980	Transferred to Turkey 1980
Samuel B. Roberts (DD 823)	December 20, 1946	FRAM I (Group B) 1962	November 2, 1970	Sunk as target 1971
Basilone (DD 824)	July 26, 1949	Prototype DDE 1949; FRAM I (Group B) 1964	November 1, 1977	Sunk as target 1982
Carpenter (DD 825)	December 15, 1949	Prototype DDK 1949; FRAM I (modified) 1965	February 20, 1981	Transferred to Turkey 1981
Agerholm (DD 826)	June 20, 1946	FRAM I (Group A) 1961	December 1, 1978	Sunk as target 1982
Robert A. Owens (DD 827)	November 5, 1949	Prototype DDK 1949; FRAM I (modified) 1964	February 22, 1982	Transferred to Turkey 1982
Timmerman (DD 828)	September 26, 1952	Last Gearing built; completed as experimental unit	July 27, 1956	Scrapped 1959
Myles C. Fox (DD 829)	March 20, 1945	DDR 1945; FRAM I (Group B) 1964	October 1, 1979	Transferred to Greece for parts 1980
Everett F. Larson (DD 830)	April 6, 1945	DDR 1945; FRAM II 1963	October 30, 1972	Transferred to South Korea 1972
Goodrich (DD 831)	April 24, 1945	DDR 1945; FRAM II 1960 (kept as DDR)	November 30, 1969	Scrapped 1977
Hanson (DD 832)	May 11, 1945	DDR 1945; FRAM I (Group B) 1964	March 31, 1973	Transferred to Taiwan 1973
Herbert J. Thomas (DD 833)	May 29, 1945	DDR 1945; FRAM I (Group B) 1965	December 4, 1970	Transferred to Taiwan 1974
Turner (DD 834)	June 12, 1945	DDR 1945; FRAM II 1960 (kept as DDR)	September 26, 1969	Scrapped 1970
Charles P. Cecil (DD 835)	June 29, 1945	DDR 1945; FRAM I (Group B) 1964	October 1, 1979	Transferred to Greece 1980
George K. Mackenzie (DD 836)	July 13, 1945	Retained 40mm guns through the 1950s; FRAM I (Group B) 1963	October 1, 1976	Sunk as target 1976
Sarsfield (DD 837)	July 31, 1945	Retained 40mm guns through the 1950s; FRAM I (Group B) 1963	October 1, 1977	Transferred to Taiwan 1977
Ernest G. Small (DD 838)	August 21, 1945	DDR 1952; FRAM II 1961	November 13, 1970	Transferred to Taiwan 1971
Power (DD 839)	September 13, 1945	FRAM I (Group B) 1962	October 1, 1977	Transferred to Taiwan 1977
Glennon (DD 840)	October 4, 1945	FRAM I (Group B) 1963	October 1, 1976	Sunk as target 1981
Noa (DD 841)	November 2, 1945	FRAM I (Group A) 1961	October 31, 1973	Transferred to Spain 1973
Fiske (DD 842)	November 28, 1945	DDR 1952; FRAM I (Group B) 1965	June 5, 1980	Transferred to Turkey 1980
Warrington (DD 843)	September 27, 1945	FRAM I (Group B) 1962	September 30, 1972	Scrapped 1973
Perry (DD 844)	January 17, 1946	FRAM I (Group A) 1960	June 30, 1973	Scrapped 1974
Baussell (DD 845)	February 7, 1946	FRAM I (Group A) 1961	May 30, 1978	Sunk as target 1987
Ozbourn (DD 846)	March 5, 1946	FRAM I (Group B) 1961	June 1, 1975	Scrapped 1975
Robert L. Wilson (DD 847)	April 25, 1946	DDE 1950; FRAM I (Group B) 1963	September 30, 1974	Sunk as target 1980
Witek (DD 848)	April 25, 1946	Completed as experimental ship; retained 40mm guns through the 1950s	August 19, 1968	Sunk as target 1969
Richard E. Kraus (DD 849)	May 23, 1946	Completed as experimental ship; FRAM I (Group B) 1964	July 1, 1976	Transferred to South Korea 1977
Joseph P. Kennedy, Jr. (DD 850)	December 15, 1945	FRAM I (Group B) 1962	July 2, 1973	Museum ship Fall River, Massachusetts
Rupertus (DD 851)	March 8, 1946	Retained 40mm guns through the 1950s; FRAM I (Group B) 1963	July 10, 1973	Transferred to Greece 1973
Leonard F. Mason (DD 852)	June 28, 1946	FRAM I (Group B) 1964	November 2, 1976	Transferred to Taiwan 1978
Charles H. Roan (DD 853)	September 2, 1946	FRAM I (Group B) 1962	September 21, 1973	Transferred to Turkey 1973

Gearing-class construction

Ship	Commissioned	Modernization	Decommissioned	Fate
Fred T. Berry (DD 858)	May 12, 1945	DDE 1949: FRAM II 1961	September 15, 1970	Sunk as reef 1972
Norris (DD 859)	June 9, 1945	DDE 1949; FRAM II 1961	December 4, 1970	Transferred to Turkey 1974
McCaffery (DD 860)	July 26, 1945	DDE 1949; FRAM II 1961	September 30, 1973	Scrapped 1974
Harwood (DD 861)	June 8, 1951	DDE 1949: FRAM II 1961	December 17, 1971	Transferred to Turkey 1971
Vogelgesang (DD 862)	April 28, 1945	FRAM I (Group B) 1962	February 23, 1982	Transferred to Mexico 1982
Steinaker (DD 863)	May 26, 1945	DDR 1953; FRAM I (Group B) 1965	February 23, 1982	Transferred to Mexico 1982
Harold J. Ellison (DD 864)	June 23, 1945	Retained 40mm guns through the 1950s; FRAM I (Group B) 1963	October 1, 1983	Transferred to Pakistan 1983
Charles R. Ware (DD 865)	July 21, 1945	FRAM I (Group B) 1962	December 12, 1974	Sunk as target 1981
Cone (DD 866)	August 18, 1945	FRAM I (Group B) 1963	October 1, 1982	Transferred to Pakistan 1982
Stribling (DD 867)	September 29, 1945	FRAM I (Group A) 1961	July 1, 1976	Sunk as target 1980
Brownson (DD 868)	November 17, 1945	FRAM I (Group B) 1964	September 30, 1976	Scrapped 1977
Arnold J. Isbell (DD 869)	January 5, 1946	Retained 40mm guns through the 1950s; FRAM I (Group B) 1962	December 4, 1973	Transferred to Greece 1973
Fechteler (DD 870)	March 2, 1946	DDR 1953; FRAM I (Group B) 1963	September 11, 1970	Scrapped 1972
Damato (DD 871)	April 27, 1946	DDE 1950; FRAM I (Group B) 1964	September 30, 1980	Transferred to Pakistan 1980
Forrest Royal (DD 872)	June 29, 1946	FRAM I (Group B) 1962	March 27, 1971	Transferred to Turkey 1971
Hawkins (DD 873)	February 10, 1945	DDR 1945; FRAM I (Group B) 1965	October 1, 1979	Transferred to Taiwan 1979
Duncan (DD 874)	February 25, 1945	DDR 1945; FRAM II 1961 (kept as DDR)	January 15, 1971	Sunk as target 1980
Henry W. Tucker (DD 875)	March 12, 1945	DDR 1945; FRAM I (Group B) 1963	December 3, 1973	Transferred to Brazil 1973
Rogers (DD 876)	March 26, 1945	DDR 1945; FRAM I (Group B) 1964	February 19, 1981	Transferred to South Korea 1981
Perkins (DD 877)	April 4, 1945	DDR 1945; FRAM II 1962	January 15, 1973	Transferred to Argentina 1973
Vesole (DD 878)	April 23, 1945	DDR 1945; FRAM I (Group B) 1964	December 1, 1976	Sunk as target 1983
Leary (DD 879)	May 7, 1945	DDR 1945; FRAM I (Group B) 1965	October 31, 1973	Transferred to Spain
Dyess (DD 880)	May 21, 1945	DDR 1945; FRAM I (Group B) 1965	February 27, 1981	Transferred to Greece for parts 1981
Bordelon (DD 881)	June 5, 1945	DDR 1945; FRAM I (Group B) 1963	July 1, 1972	Transferred to Iran for parts 1977
Furse (DD 882)	July 10, 1945	DDR 1945; FRAM I (Group B) 1963	August 31, 1972	Transferred to Spain
Newman K. Perry (DD 883)	July 26, 1945	DDR 1945; FRAM I (Group B) 1965	February 27, 1981	Transferred to South Korea 1981
Floyd B. Parks (DD 884)	August 31, 1945	FRAM I (Group B) 1963	July 2, 1973	Scrapped 1974
John R. Craig (DD 885)	August 20, 1945	FRAM I (Group B) 1963	July 27, 1979	Sunk as target 1980
Orleck (DD 886)	September 15, 1945	Retained 40mm guns through the 1950s; FRAM I (Group B) 1963	October 1, 1982	Transferred to Turkey 1982; currently museum ship in Orange, Texas
Brinkley Bass (DD 887)	October 1, 1945	FRAM I (Group B) 1962	December 3, 1973	Transferred to Brazil 1973
Stickell (DD 888)	October 31, 1945	DDR 1953; FRAM I (Group B) 1964	July 1, 1972	Transferred to Greece 1972
O'Hare (DD 889)	November 29, 1945	DDR 1953; FRAM I (Group B) 1963	October 31, 1973	Transferred to Spain 1973
Meredith (DD 890)	December 31, 1945	FRAM I (Group A) 1961	June 29, 1979	Transferred to Turkey 1979

Gearing-class specifications

Displacement	2,425 tons standard; 3,410–3,520 tons full load
Dimensions	Length 390ft, 6in; beam 40ft, 10in; draft 19ft
Machinery	2 shafts making 60,000shp
Performance	34.5kt (design); actual 31.3kt (1962); 4,000nm at 20kt
Crew	281–307

This is *Norfolk* after being refitted with the troubled 3in/70 twin mount. Also visible are the ship's four Weapon Alphas, two forward and two aft. With its clipper bow, large superstructure, and two uneven stacks, the ship projects a graceful appearance.

Norfolk class

To contend with the potential threat of a Soviet submarine force built around a Soviet version of the German Type XXI high-speed submarine, the USN began design work on a "Submarine Killer Ship." Such a ship had to be large to mount the elaborate sonar suite planned and possess the speed and endurance to operate even in the rough weather of the Atlantic. The heavy ASW battery had to be able to mount multiple attacks. AAW was a secondary consideration, but it was intended that the ship carry the new 3in/70 twin mounts.

In February 1947, a design based on the hull of the Atlanta-class antiaircraft cruiser was selected for development. As built, *Norfolk* projected a powerful and balanced appearance with a large superstructure, two stacks, and a clipper bow. The new design was classified as a CLK (sub-killer cruiser) to reflect its unique mission and capabilities.

The lead ship was included in the FY 48 program. The total cost of almost $62 million forced the cancelation of a second unit in 1951. After the CLK classification was dropped in 1951, *Norfolk* reverted to a DL. The ship proved to be a white elephant and was used for experimental purposes

THE BIG DESTROYERS

1. *Mitscher* as built. *Mitscher* was the lead ship in a class of four. These ships were the largest USN destroyers ever at almost 500ft in length. This view shows *Mitscher* as built in 1953. With two 5in/54 single mounts and two twin 3in/50 the ship appears underarmed. The original ASW suite was highlighted by two Weapon Alphas fitted near the 3in/50 mounts. Note the large SPS-8 height-finding radar located aft of second stack which allowed the ship to function as a picket.

2. *Norfolk* in 1959. The unique *Norfolk* was a cruiser-sized ASW ship. This is a view from 1959 when the ship finally received its four 3in/70 mounts. To perform in its role as an ASW hunter-killer, the ship was fitted with four Weapon Alphas and eight fixed torpedo tubes in the aft superstructure. Both the 3in/70 and the Weapon Alpha proved to be a failure. With its limited capabilities, *Norfolk* was retired early after a brief career as an experimental ship.

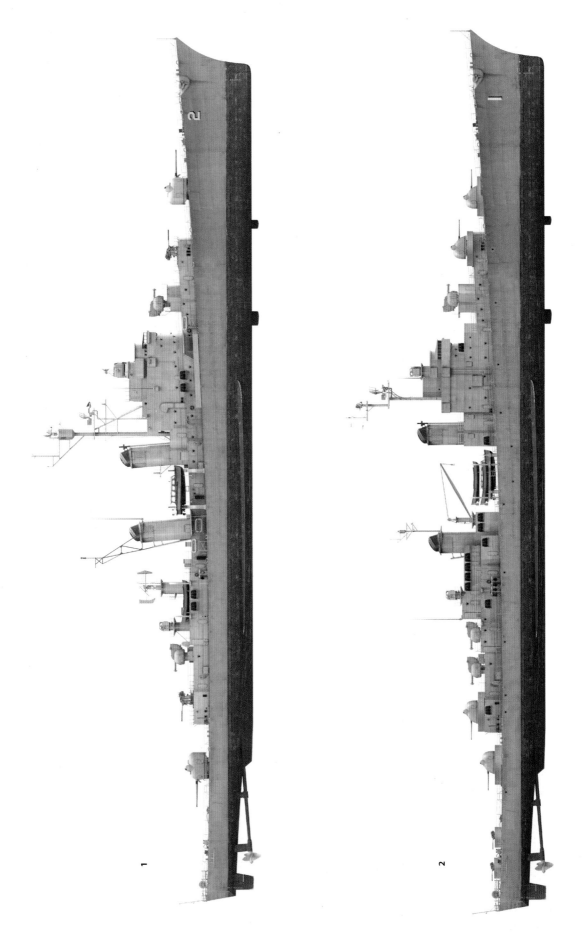

evaluating sonars and ASROC, among other equipment. Consideration was given to converting the large ship into a missile frigate, but this gained no traction and the ship was retired early in 1970.

Norfolk-class construction

Ship	Commissioned	Modernization	Decommissioned	Fate
Norfolk (CLK 1, later DL 1)	March 4, 1953	None	January 15, 1970	Scrapped 1974

As commissioned, the ship carried four 3in/50 mounts and four Weapon Alphas, split evenly fore and aft. Sixteen 20mm guns and eight fixed torpedo tubes were also fitted. The only major modification during its career was the removal of the useless 20mm guns and the replacement of the 3in/50 mounts with the much larger and enclosed 3in/70 mounts by 1959 and the replacement of the two aft Weapon Alphas with an ASROC launcher in 1960.

Norfolk-class specifications

Displacement	5,600 tons standard; 7,041 tons full load
Dimensions	Length 540ft; beam 54ft; draft 27ft
Machinery	2 shafts making 80,000shp
Performance	32.5kt; 6,000nm at 20kt
Crew	540

Mitscher was converted into a guided-missile destroyer between 1966 and 1968. This is *Mitscher* photographed at Souda Bay, Crete after its conversion. The conversion was extensive and added an ASROC launcher forward and a Mk 13 SAM launcher aft. Note the two SPG-51 target illuminators abaft the second stack and the SPS-48 3-D radar on the aft trellis mast. Carrier *America* is in the background.

Mitscher class

These were large and expensive ships, thus only four were built beginning in 1949. They were maximized for ASW and AAW. All ships were completed with the standard 3in/50 mounts but received the 3in/70 mounts when they became available. The original ASW suite was extensive with two Weapon Alphas, four fixed torpedo tubes, facilities for firing lightweight homing

This is *John S. McCain* in 1976 following its conversion into a guided-missile destroyer. The conversion of the last two ships in the class was canceled because of cost. After completing its conversion in 1969, *John S. McCain* served only a few years until being decommissioned in 1978.

torpedoes, a depth charge rack on the stern, and two Hedgehog launchers. They carried the SPS-8 height-finding radar so were fully capable of acting as picket ships.

The ships in this class were bedeviled by their new machinery being the first ships to carry the 1,200lb 950-degree boilers. These were lightweight and were designed to develop 80,000shp. However, the new machinery proved unreliable and contributed to the early decommissioning of these ships.

Between 1960 and 1962, all four ships received an ASW upgrade. The short-ranged and ineffective Weapon Alpha was removed and a flight deck and hangar was fitted aft for the DASH. Mk 32 triple torpedo tubes were also added. The last two ships in the class were the first to carry the new SQS-26 sonar.

Mitscher-class construction				
Ship	Commissioned	Modernization	Decommissioned	Fate
Mitscher (DL 2)	May 16, 1953	ASW upgrade 1960–62; converted to DDG 1966–68 (reclassified DDG-35)	June 1, 1978	Scrapped 1980
John S. McCain (DL 3)	October 12, 1953	ASW upgrade 1960–62; converted to DDG 1966–68 (reclassified DDG-36)	April 29, 1978	Scrapped 1979
Willis A. Lee (DL 4)	September 28, 1954	ASW upgrade 1960–62	December 20, 1969	Scrapped 1973
Wilkinson (DL 5)	July 29, 1954	ASW upgrade 1960–62	December 19, 1969	Scrapped 1975

It was planned to convert all four ships to DDGs, but after this work was completed on the first two ships, conversion of the other two ships was canceled because of cost. Their lack of capability and the cost of the Vietnam War led to the last two ships in the class being decommissioned early in 1969.

Mitscher and *John S. McCain* were converted into DDGs, prolonging their careers until 1978. A single-armed Mk 13 Tartar launcher was fitted aft with a magazine for 40 missiles. Two trellis masts were added with the aft one carrying the SPS-48 3-D radar for the missile system. Two SPG-51s were

John Paul Jones photographed at high speed while running sea trials on March 25, 1956. High speed was a design emphasis of this class but they produced a disappointing 33kt. *John Paul Jones* was later converted into a guided-missile destroyer and was one of the longest-serving Forrest Sherman-class ships being decommissioned in 1982.

fitted for target illumination. In addition, an ASROC launcher was added forward of the bridge. Following this conversion, the only guns remaining were the two single 5in/54 mounts. This conversion was extensive and changed the appearance of the ships dramatically.

Mitscher-class specifications	
Displacement	3,500 tons standard; 4,730 tons full load (5,200 as AAW conversion)
Dimensions	Length 493ft; beam 50ft; draft 21ft
Machinery	2 shafts making 80,000shp
Performance	33–35kt; 4,000nm at 20kt
Crew	440 (377 as AAW conversion)

Forrest Sherman class

What began as a design for a mass-produced mobilization destroyer resulted in a very traditional destroyer design with a heavy gun armament. Beginning

 THE FORREST SHERMAN CLASS

1. An all-gun ship in 1972. The Forrest Sherman class was the last USN all-gun destroyer and certainly its best-looking one. The top view shows *Edson* in 1972 after it had received a slight modernization. The ship projects a clean and balanced appearance with its high freeboard forward, two stacks, and three 5in/54 Mk 42 mounts. Only the aft 3in/50 mount remains, the forward one having been removed. On the later ships in the class, the Mk 68 fire control director was moved to the forward position and the Mk 56 director to the aft position, as shown here. ASW weaponry consists of Hedgehog launchers forward of the bridge and two Mk 32 torpedo launchers abaft the forward stack. The ship carries a SPS-37 air search radar and a SPS-10 surface search radar on the foremast.

2. A Forrest Sherman guided-missile destroyer in 1968. In the bottom view, *Somers* is shown in 1968 after its conversion into a DDG. Only four Forrest Shermans received this modernization which changed their appearance dramatically. All the previous armament was removed with the exception of the forward 5in/54 mount; the Mk 32 torpedo launchers were moved to a position forward of the bridge. The Tartar SAM launcher can be seen aft. Its supporting target illuminator (SPG-51) was placed on a new deckhouse, and the new SPS-48 3-D radar can be seen on the trellis mast built around the second stack. Abaft the second stack is an ASROC launcher. The radars on the foremast are a SPS-40 and a SPS-10. Overall, this was a considerable investment for minimal additional capabilities.

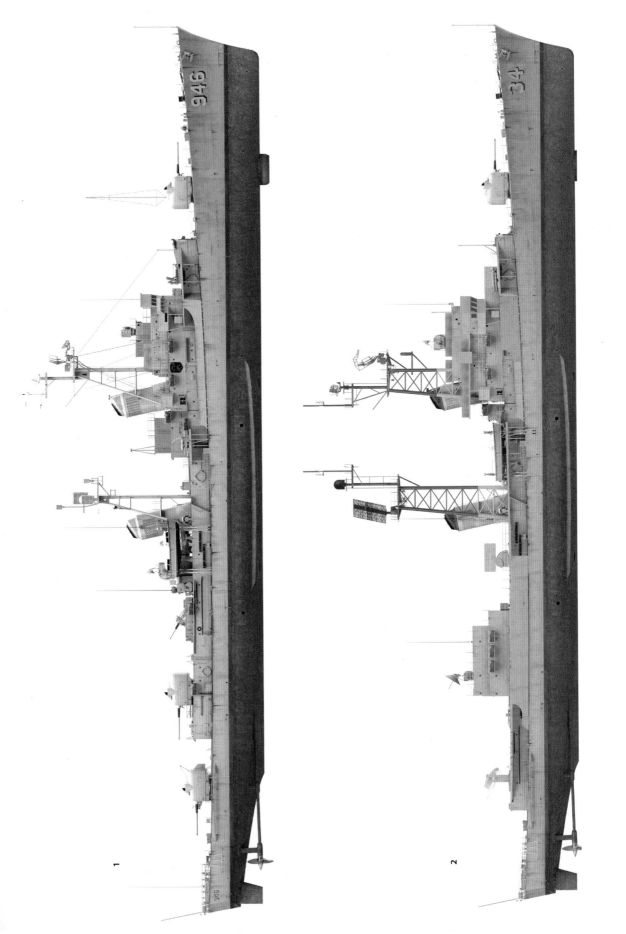

1

2

in 1953 when the lead ship *Forrest Sherman* was laid down, 18 ships were placed into commission by 1959. The USN's last class of all gun destroyers carried three single 5in/54 and two 3in/50 mounts. ASW weaponry was limited to depth charges, two fixed Hedgehogs, and four torpedo tubes capable of firing homing weapons.

Speed was also a design focus. With machinery capable of developing 70,000shp, a top speed of 33kt could be attained. Later ships of the class were completed with increased freeboard forward to deal with the wetness prevalent on the Fletcher/Sumner/Gearing designs. This, and the balanced appearance of the two stacks and three gun mounts, gave the ship appealing aesthetics.

Even before the entire class was completed, the USN wanted to convert all 18 ships into DDGs. This was a very expensive plan and was quashed by the then Secretary of Defense. Eventually, only four ships were modernized in this manner. A Tartar launcher was fitted aft and a SPG-51 placed atop a deckhouse aft. Since only one target illuminator was fitted, the system could only engage a single target at a time. The SPS-48 3-D radar was fitted on a large mast built around the second stack. All the guns were removed except the forward 5in/54 mount. The ASW capabilities remained significant with an ASROC launcher and two triple Mk 32 launchers in front of the bridge.

After the cancelation of the DDG scheme, eight ships were modified to enhance their ASW capabilities. One 5in/54 mount was removed and replaced by an ASROC launcher. This took place between 1967 and 1972. The Hedgehogs and the 3in/50 guns were also removed. In addition to the ASROC launcher, two Mk 32 launchers were fitted. ASW sensors were enhanced with an SQS-23 bow-mounted sonar and an SQS-35 VDS on the stern.

Some of the ships remained largely unmodified during their careers. They did receive the hull-mounted SQS-23. By the end of their careers, only the 5in/54 mounts remained. The only ASW weaponry was a pair of Mk 32 torpedo launchers mounted on the forward superstructure.

This fine view of *Somers* from June 1971 shows a Forrest Sherman-class ship in a guided-missile destroyer configuration. The entire aft portion of the ship is devoted to the Tartar SAM system. Note the single SPG-51 target illuminator on the large aft deck house. ASW weaponry included the ASROC launcher amidships and the Mk 32 torpedo tubes forward. Only one of the original 5in/54 mounts remains.

Davis was one of eight ships given an ASW modernization late in their careers. *Davis* received this work in 1969–70 during which it was fitted with an ASROC launcher aft in place of a 5in/54 mount and a SQS-35 VDS on its fantail. The ineffective 3in/50 mounts were removed and the new SPS-40 air search radar was added.

Forrest Sherman-class construction

Ship	Commissioned	Modernization	Decommissioned	Fate
Forrest Sherman (DD 931)	November 9, 1955	None	November 5, 1982	Scrapped 2014
John Paul Jones (DD 932)	April 5, 1956	Converted to DDG 1965–67 (reclassified DDG-32)	December 15, 1982	Sunk as target 2001
Barry (DD 933)	July 9, 1956	ASW upgrade 1967–68	November 5, 1982	Museum ship Washington, DC 1984–2015; scrapped 2022
Decatur (DD 936)	December 7, 1956	Converted to DDG 1966–67 (reclassified DDG-31)	June 30, 1983	Sunk as target 2004
Davis (DD 937)	March 6, 1957	ASW upgrade 1969–70	December 20, 1982	Scrapped 1994
Jonas Ingram (DD 938)	July 19, 1957	ASW upgrade 1969–70	March 4, 1983	Sunk as target 1988
Manley (DD 940)	February 1, 1957	ASW upgrade 1970–71	March 4, 1983	Scrapped 1994
DuPont (DD 941)	July 1, 1957	ASW upgrade 1969–70	March 4, 1983	Scrapped 1993
Bigelow (DD 942)	November 8, 1957	None	November 5, 1982	Sunk as target 2003
Blandy (DD 943)	November 26, 1957	ASW upgrade 1969–70	November 5, 1982	Scrapped 1994
Mullinix (DD 944)	March 7, 1958	None	August 11, 1983	Sunk as target 1992
Hull (DD 945)	July 3, 1958	None	July 11, 1983	Sunk as target 1998
Edson (DD 946)	November 7, 1958	None	December 15, 1988	Museum ship in Bay City, Michigan
Somers (DD 947)	April 3, 1959	Converted to DDG 1966–68 (reclassified DDG-34)	November 19, 1982	Sunk as target 1998
Morton (DD 948)	May 26, 1959	ASW upgrade 1969–70	November 22, 1982	Scrapped 1992
Parsons (DD 949)	October 29, 1959	Converted to DDG 1966–67 (reclassified DDG-33)	November 19, 1983	Sunk as target 1989
Richard S. Edwards (DD 950)	February 5, 1959	ASW upgrade 1970–71	November 22, 1982	Sunk as target 1991
Turner Joy (DD 951)	August 3, 1959	None	November 22, 1982	Museum ship in Bremerton, Washington

Of note, the last seven ships built switched the position of the fire control directors. The first ships placed the larger Mk 37 abaft the second stack and the smaller and less capable Mk 56 on the forward superstructure. The last seven ships reversed these positions. Only the first two ships received the fixed tubes. The remainder were fitted with equipment to drop the Mk 32 homing torpedo.

Hull was the only USN destroyer to carry an 8in gun. Between 1975 and 1978, an experimental 8in/55 Mk 71 was mounted in the forward position for a series of tests to determine whether a destroyer could carry such a heavy weapon. Though promising, it was eventually terminated in favor of a 5in/54 firing Rocket Assisted Projectiles.

Forrest Sherman-class specifications (as completed)	
Displacement	2,850 tons standard; 4,050 tons full load (4,150 as AAW conversion)
Dimensions	Length 418ft; beam 45ft; draft 22ft
Machinery	2 shafts making 70,000shp
Performance	33kt; 4,500nm at 20kt
Crew	337 (later 292; 307 as ASW modification; 335 as AAW conversion)

Kenneth D. Bailey photographed in the Mediterranean Sea on June 24, 1968. It was one of six Gearings to retain its DDR classification after receiving FRAM work as evinced by the presence of the SPS-30 height-finding radar on the aft deckhouse. These ships were some of the few Gearings to receive FRAM II work – note the absence of an ASROC launcher amidships and the presence of three 5in/38 mounts and a VDS on the fantail.

ANALYSIS AND CONCLUSION

During the Cold War, USN operations were centered on its carriers. These were protected by virtually all other components of the fleet, including a large number of highly sophisticated guided missile cruisers and destroyers. But during the early phases of the Cold War these impressive missile-armed combatants did not exist. Carrier escort duties were performed predominantly by the gun destroyers built during and in the immediate aftermath of World War II. Facing no expected opposition from enemy surface fleets, these ships were expected to provide ASW and AAW protection to the fleet. As they were modernized, first in the 1950s and later during the massive FRAM

program in the early 1960s, the Fletcher, Sumner, and Gearing classes were increasingly focused on ASW.

Fletcher-class destroyers were excellent ships when first produced, but because they did not compare favorably to the subsequent Sumner and Gearing classes, they were not heavily modernized during the Cold War. Had the Soviets built a massive submarine fleet during the first stages of the Cold War, the USN would have invested in the ASW modernizations of large numbers of Fletchers as a counter. Even though they were not extensively modernized, the Fletchers still proved useful as mobilization reserves. Since they were not modernized, the Fletchers were the least overweight of the war-built classes and had the highest sustained speed and the best acceleration. They proved useful during the Korean conflict as shore bombardment platforms.

The USN preferred the Sumner and Gearing classes because of their powerful six-gun main batteries. Being somewhat larger than the Fletchers, the Gearings were also better able to receive modernization. All existing Sumners and Gearings were in service during the Korean War – an impressive total of 151 units. Almost all of these ships were modernized in some way and most received a FRAM rebuild. They served extensively off Korea and Vietnam in shore bombardment roles during which many were damaged by artillery, mines, or even aircraft. The iconic gun destroyer of the Cold War is a modernized Gearing-class destroyer.

However, modernization of the Sumner and Gearing classes was only partially effective. Though they remained excellent shore bombardment

Alfred A. Cunningham pictured on August 9, 1964 following the completion of its FRAM II modernization. Almost all surviving Sumners received this modernization which allowed them to remain in service into the 1970s. FRAM II was primarily an ASW upgrade.

DuPont was another Forrest Sherman ship to receive the ASW modernization. Following the cancelation of the DDG conversion, the other 14 ships in the class were scheduled to get this upgrade, but only eight were eventually modernized due to costs. This is *DuPont* in 1978 during Unitas XIX.

platforms by virtue of their four or six 5in/38 guns, in other warfare areas they were more limited. As even the USN recognized, by the late 1950s, the 5in and 3in guns on destroyers were ineffective against modern air targets. This left USN gun destroyers virtually undefended against air and missile attack. The same vulnerability held true against modern submarines. ASW exercises during the early Cold War period found USN destroyers ineffective in detecting submarines; when a detection was made, ASW weapons of the period were inadequate.

The USN's first attempt to build an ultimate gun destroyer ended in failure since the Mitscher class was too expensive for mass production. The class began the trend of mounting fewer, but more capable weapons. Placing only two 5in guns on a large destroyer resulted in an apparently under-armed ship, but the new guns were automatic and were equal to a 5in/38 main battery twice as large. The ships sacrificed gun firepower to mount a significant ASW capability and this led to criticism that they sacrificed too much firepower for ASW capability.

The Fletcher, Sumner, and Gearing classes lacked the top speed desired by the USN and all three were notoriously wet. The forward turret of the Sumner and Gearing classes was continually subjected to damage from heavy seas. This prompted the USN to build a new-design gun destroyer with high speed and heavier firepower. The resulting Forrest Sherman class handled well and possessed good seakeeping qualities, but the day of the all-gun destroyer had passed. These ships were already obsolescent when they were designed. Beginning in FY 57, construction of a new class of missile destroyer was begun on the modified hull of the Forrest Sherman class.

FURTHER READING

Bruhn, David D. and Mathews, Richard S., *On the Gunline* (Berwyn Heights, MD: Heritage Books, 2019).

Cagle, Malcolm W. and Manson, Frank A., *The Sea War in Korea* (Annapolis, MD: Naval Institute Press, 1957).

Conway's All the World's Fighting Ships 1947–1995 (Annapolis, MD: Naval Institute Press, 1995).

Dictionary of American Naval Fighting Ships, found at the Navy History and Heritage Command website.

Friedman, Norman, *Naval Radar* (London: Conway Maritime Press, 1981).

Friedman, Norman, *The Naval Institute Guide to World Naval Weapons Systems* (Annapolis, MD: Naval Institute Press, 1991).

Friedman, Norman, *US Destroyers* (Annapolis, MD: Naval Institute Press, 2004).

Jane's Fighting Ships (various editions from 1959 to 1980).

King, Randolph W. (ed.), *Naval Engineering and American Sea Power* (Baltimore, MD: The Nautical & Aviation Publishing Company of America, nd).

Lott, Arnold S., *USS Joseph P. Kennedy, JR. (DD 850)* (Annapolis: Leeward Publications, 1979).

Marolda, Edward J. (ed.), *The US Navy in the Korean War* (Annapolis, MD: Naval Institute Press, 2007).

Muir, Malcolm, *Black Shoes and Blue Water* (Washington: Naval Historical Center, 1996).

Pretty, R.T. (ed.), *Jane's Weapon Systems*, 7th edition (New York: Franklin Watts Inc., 1975).

Ross, Al, *The Destroyer, The Sullivans* (Annapolis, MD: Naval Institute Press, 1988).

Silverstone, Paul H., *US Warships Since 1945* (Annapolis, MD: Naval Institute Press, 1987).

Silverstone, Paul H., *The Navy of the Nuclear Age 1947–2007* (New York: Routledge, 2009).

Sumrall, Robert F., *USS Laffey (DD-724)* (Somerset, MA: Tin Can Sailors, 2001).

Sumrall, Robert F., *Sumner-Gearing-Class Destroyers* (Annapolis, MD: Naval Institute Press, 1995).

Sumrall, Robert F. and Walkowiak, Thomas F., *USS Kidd (DD661)* (Missoula, MT: Pictorial Histories Publishing Company, 1989).

The Ships and Aircraft of the US Fleet, 9th–14th editions (Annapolis, MD: Naval Institute Press).

INDEX

Page numbers in **bold** refer to plate captions, pictures and illustrations.